MW01206575

Cruise IN:
A guide to Indiana's automotive past and present

by
Dennis E. Horvath
and Terri Horvath

First Edition

Publishing Resources,
A division of TRG-The Resource Group
Indianapolis, Indiana

Cruise IN:

A guide to Indiana's automotive past and present

by Dennis E. Horvath and Terri Horvath

Published by Publishing Resources
a division of TRG-The Resource Group
9220 N. College Avenue
Indianapolis, IN 46240-1031

ISBN 0-9644364-2-6

cover photo: *Intraplanetary Space Vehicle 1936*
copyright 1982 Dennis E. Horvath

Table of Contents

Introduction

Elwood Haynes' *The Complete Motorist*, published in 1913, isn't like a typical owner's manual found in today's glove compartments. The publication also pays homage to the possibilities and responsibility of operating an automobile. His functional yet romantic outlook regarding the automobile also reflects society's continuing love affair. We have found that the automobile provides some of our best and worst memories--our first taste of freedom along with adult responsibilities--our legacy and future dreams.

For life-long Hoosiers and temporary transplants, mementos of this long-term relationship with the automobile are scattered throughout Indiana in museums, historical markers, remnants of manufacturing plants and events that beckon auto devotees. These provide the sights, legends, facts and figures that still captivate our interest and provide the foundation of this book.

Cruise IN serves as both a tour guide and a short historical accounting of various communities' connection with auto manufacturing.

More than 40 Indiana cities and towns have either had automobiles manufactured or assembled in their borders. In addition, more than 200 automobiles, trucks and cyclecars can claim Indiana production or assemblage, which is more than 6 percent of the approximate 2,500 vehicles produced in the United States. Names like Auburn, Cord, Duesenberg and Studebaker have lent distinction to Indiana's automotive past and present. Others may be more obscure, but have also played important, innovative roles in the development of the automobile. In fact, Indiana can claim many automotive firsts, milestones that are listed on the following pages.

This book also looks at the rise and fall of automobile manufacturing in Indiana, current major attractions and little-known sites and provides a calendar of annual auto-related events.

The section entitled On the Road reviews various communities' historical connection, and any local sights immediately follow the town's history under Roadside attractions. Scattered throughout the pages are stories of automotive pioneers and their creations under the title Behind the wheel. A summary of milestones in Indiana's automotive history is followed by two lists of Indiana-built autos sorted by city and model name.

Cruise IN is not intended to be the definitive textbook on the state's automotive history. Instead, the purpose is to serve as a companion to the motorist who wants to explore Indiana's contributions to the automobile.

We have enjoyed cruisin' Indiana and hope that the following information helps you in your journeys.

Acknowledgments

We wish to thank the many individuals whose foresight and hard-work resulted in the museums and automotive data collections at the Auburn Cord Duesenberg Museum, the Henry Ford Museum and the National Automotive History Collection at the Detroit Public Library. Without their efforts, we may not have had the resources available to produce this book.

Thanks also to a group of individuals who provided their assistance during the research phase of this book: Leigh Darbee, Wilma Gibbs and Susan Sutton, collection specialists, the Indiana Historical Society; David Lewis, Indiana Section of the Indiana State Library; Henry Blommel, automotive historian, Connersville; Gregg Buttermore, publicist, and John Emery, archivist, the Auburn Cord Duesenberg Museum; Michelle Bottorff, director, and Jim Waechter, curator, the Wayne County Historical Museum; Kay Frazer, director, Elwood Haynes Museum, David N. Lewis, research assistant, the Vigo County Public Library; June Potter, director, Randolph County Promotion and Visitors Bureau; Judie Silvers, executive director, North Manchester Chamber of Commerce; and friends Bob and Mary Kraft, who have accompanied us on our journey exploring Indiana's automotive history.

Why Indiana? Why not?

Indiana's plentiful supply of lumber lured several industries into its borders, including the makers of carriages and wagons during the mid to late 1800s. The automobile industry in the early 1900s was a natural offspring of carriage manufacturers, which could provide not just parts but the skilled labor as well.

The growth spurt between 1910 and 1920 separated the nation's auto makers into two groups–the mass-produced auto giants and the craftsmen. Most of Indiana's auto makers chose to be craftsmen and purchased automotive parts and assembled them by hand. As a result, these companies were small, and many became known for producing high-class and high-priced cars. Nearly every one of the Indiana cars that became well-known were in this catagory, including names like Duesenberg, Cord, Stutz and Cole, appealed to the upper end of the consumer market.

Until about 1920, there seemed to enough demand for both the mass-produced and high-quality cars. However, a series of economic factors at this time helped contribute to the decline of Hoosier auto making. Price slashing and an expansion-crazed environment trapped Indiana manufacturers in a philsophical battle with the Michigan titans. Hoosiers were ill-prepared for this kind of competition, and most wanted to remain craftsmen choosing to concentrate on higher priced vehicles instead of diversifying. Plus, the economic recession during this time added more financial burdens on the population, which became increasingly interested in the mass-produced auto. And Michigan had the financial backers willing to commit financial resources to give the state's auto manufacturing the boost it needed. The Hoosier financial community generally proved to be of little assitance to its own local automobile industry.

Studebaker was the lone survivor of the depression, continuing production until 1963.

However, the 1980s and 1990s have introduced a revival, evident in the introduction of the Mishawaka-produced Hummers and the Lafayette-produced Subarus, Isuzus and Hondas. Toyota also has plans in southern Indiana, and Chyrsler has reinforced its presence in Kokomo.

Early Indiana statistics

- The 1900 census ranked Indiana seventh by the number of automobile manufacturers and wage earners and ninth by value of product.

- The 1905 census shows Indiana contirbuted 6 percent of the industry's total national value of product.

- In 1909 Indiana was the second largest producer (13.1 percent) of the nation's automobiles after Michigan (51.1 percent).

- In 1910 General Motors had controlling interest in 20 automobile and parts companies.

- In 1914, Indiana produced 5.7 percent of the nation's automotive parts. The census showed 38 automotive manufacturers and 48 body and parts manufacturers.

- Between 1910 and 1920 in the United States, the number of automobiles produced by each auto worker rose from 1.68 to 5.52.

- In 1910, automobiles costing less than $1,000 comprised 30 percent of the market. By 1916, the number rose to 82 percent.

- In 1919, the number of Indiana auto manufacturers fell to 27. In 1921, the number dwindled to 10.

Indiana today and tomorrow

The question: Where does Indiana stand regarding the automotive industry today?

The answer: Indiana is alive and well, producing autos and sport utility vehicles at Subaru Isuzu Automotive, Inc., in Lafayette; trucks and sport utility vehicles at General Motors Truck & Bus Group in Fort Wayne; and off-road vehicles and military vehicles at AM General Corporation in Mishawaka. Plus the Toyota's North American Truck Plant in Princeton should be operational by the turn of the century.

And that is only part of the answer. Indiana is a leading producer of automotive components, electronics, and parts. In fact, if you drive an American automobile, there is an excellent chance that a good part of it is made in Indiana. For instance, all Chrysler auto transmissions are manufactured in Kokomo.

The automotive components, electronics, and parts industries break down into eleven categories: auto fabrics trim; plastic parts; auto stampings; internal combustion engines; carburetors, pistons, piston rings, & valves; vehicular lighting; electronic components and electrical equipment for internal combustion engines; storage batteries; motor vehicle and car bodies; truck and bus bodies; and motor vehicle parts and accessories.

Indiana employment accounts for a large share of American auto parts workers.

Other facts:
- Cummins Engine Co. is the nation's leading diesel engine manufacturer.
- Lafayette's Subaru Isuzu plant produces 240,000 vehicles annually.
- The General Motors Truck & Bus Group assembly plant in Fort Wayne produces a vehicle a minute.
- Zollner Pistons is the number one piston manufacturer in Indiana. (Sidenote: The Fort Wayne Zollner Pistons was the predecessor of the NBA Detroit Pistons.)
- Seven of the top 10 auto parts employers are represented by General Motors Corporation, Ford Motor Company, and Chrysler Corporation. The "Big Three" continue to invest in Indiana.

ON THE ROAD

Cruising into the communities that made automotive history in Indiana

Who's on First?

Who developed the first automobile in America? It's a question that has been discussed thoroughly. Although a group of native Hoosiers and long-time residents lay claim to the title, most historians agree that the auto in America emerged naturally as the requisite technology developed. It was probably developed concurrently by individuals working independently on the "horseless carriage." Suitable gasoline internal combustion engines were not available in the U.S. until late 1880's or early 1990's.

But when historians must name a title holder, generally they point to J. Frank and Charles E. Duryea. By Frank's account, they produced their first operable machine in Springfield, Massachusetts. A contemporary story in the town's newspaper *The Republican*, September 22, 1893, confirms the initial, rather disappointing test run. In 1896, they used the same design to manufacture, which is accepted as the start of the commercial auto industry in America. Their Duryea Motor Wagon Company failed in 1898.

It is a well-documented fact that Elwood Haynes of Kokomo successfully demonstrated his "Pioneer" automobile on July 4, 1894. This run preceded commercial production of Haynes-Apperson automobiles by two years. With the failure of the Duryea firm, Haynes was recognized as the proprietor and inventive genius behind the oldest automobile company in America.

Charles H. Black drove a German-made Benz around Indianapolis in 1891, probably one of the first automobiles driven in the country. His construction of a Black automobile at any time predating the above events has not been established. No contemporary newspaper accounts exist to corroborate his claims.

An 1960 article in *Antique Automobile* and an entry in the *Encyclopedia Britanica* credited John W. Lambert with building America's first successful automobile in 1891 while he was a resident of Ohio City, Ohio (just across the state line, south east of Decatur, Indiana). This predated both the Duryea and Haynes claims of the first American auto. Lambert may not have pressed his claim because he felt that although extremely successful mechanically, it was a financial failure because he was unable to generate sufficient sales to build it.

So please—don't shoot the messenger. We aren't choosing favorites.

Anderson

Automobile manufacturing lasted 23 years in Anderson with about 19 different models built here between 1898 and 1921, starting with the Buckeye Gas Buggy. No manufacturing buildings remain from this era.

However, the home of one of Buckeye's first innovators, John W. Lambert, still stands on the southwest corner of Hendricks and West 7th streets. He moved to Anderson in 1894 to oversee operations at the Buckeye Manufacturing Company, a gas engine manufacturer. By 1898, the Buckeye engine was fitted to a four-wheel buggy and operated with some success. In 1905, Lambert formed the Lambert Automobile Division of Buckeye, which operated in Anderson for 12 years.

John W. Lambert is considered the father of the friction-drive transmission and completed it in 1897. Lambert also had over 600 patents in the automobile, gasoline engine and other mechanical fields. Lambert was a long-time Anderson resident and is buried in the East Maplewood Cemetery. (Additional information on Lambert is in the Union City section.)

The arrival in 1908 of the DeTamble Automobile Company was the result of a community effort. To encourage outside industry to relocate in Anderson, a booster movement was formed to implement a search. The committee lured the DeTamble from Indianapolis on the prospect that it would hire 600 employees for its new automobile plant. The company received a $50,000 bonus to construct its facility at 1200 East 32nd Street. The DeTamble Company operated in Anderson through 1912.

Also in 1908, another company to receive support from the Anderson booster committee was the Rider-Lewis Motor Company. The firm moved from Muncie to a site at Second and Sycamore Streets. Ralph Lewis designed the car, and George D. Rider financed the operations. In March of 1911, the factory was sold to the Nyberg Automobile Works. Anderson operations ceased in 1912.

Between 1907 and 1910 the Anderson Carriage Company built the Anderson, fashioned after a buggy from top to bed but with heavy wheels made with soft cushion tires. The Model B Anderson had a two-cylinder, 12-hp, air-cooled engine. Completely equipped, the modest sum was $525.

In 1914, came the Caesar and the Pneumobile, which featured four shock absorbers in place of springs of any kind. The Laurel Motors Corporation produced the Laurel between 1917 and 1919.

The Madison Motors Company produced the Madison (1915-1919) and the Dolly Madison (1915). The Madison featured seven- and five-passenger touring cars and a two-passenger roadster.

There are numerous other short-lived makes that were built in Anderson. Most vanished after a short time without a trace.

Today Anderson is a center for electrical equipment for internal combustion engines (Delphi Energy & Engine Management Systems Division of General Motors, formerly Delco-Remy Division of General Motors). Vehicular lighting is represented by Delphi Interior & Lighting Systems, Division of General Motors, formerly The Guide Lamp Division of General Motors. Anderson is also one of the leading electromechanical technology centers in the world.

The town's current status was spurred by the Remy brothers, Frank and Perry, who developed a high-tension magneto used on the 1905 Buick. In 1909, the Remys sold more magnetos than all other competitors combined. United Motors bought Remy Electric Company and its chief rival Dayton Engineering Laboratories Company in 1916. The Delco-Remy merger under GM took place in 1918. Delco-Remy Plant One at 2401 Columbus Avenue is still in use.

The Guide Lamp division became part of GM in 1928, and Plant One is housed in a building at 25th Street and Arrow Avenue. The original plant that produced all the headlights for GM vehicles was less than one acre under roof. Guide Lamp introduced plastic taillight lenses in 1947 and has continued to develop plastics for the automotive industry. Delphi Interior & Lighting Systems Division is distinguished as the world's largest producer of automotive lighting and a leading producer of plastic (soft face) bumper systems.

Did you know?

According to local legend, the nation's first traffic light was installed in downtown Carmel in 1923. Leslie Haines invented the device which was eight-feet tall and had one red and one green light.

Roadside attractions

A historical marker on the southwest corner of 12th & Meridian streets marks the site of the Remy brothers' first facility.

The Delco Remy Plant One Complex is located at 2401 Columbus.

John Lambert's former home is on the southwest corner of Hendricks and W. 7th streets. A historical marker is in the front.

The Anderson Speedway hosts the popular Little 500 as well as other races during the season beginning in mid-April.
1311 Pendleton Avenue, 765-642-0206, call for a complete schedule

The Nickleson Library archives at Anderson University contains the personal papers of C.E. Wilson, secretary of defense during the Eisenhower administration and president of General Motors from 1941-1953.
Anderson University, 1100 E. 5th Street, 765-641-4286
(649-4284 for archives), call for appointment

Auburn

During its 37 years in the auto manufacturing limelight, Auburn produced about 15 different models, from Auburn to Zimmerman. Two of these, Auburn and Cord, are highly sought after by collectors and enthusiasts alike. In fact, the chance to view these and hundreds of other cars draws thousands of enthusiasts each year to visit the Auburn Cord Duesenberg Museum and attend the annual Auburn Cord Duesenberg Festival on Labor Day weekend.

Appropriately, Auburn's automotive history starts with the Auburn Automobile Company.

In 1896, control of the Eckhart Carriage Company was turned over to the Eckhart brothers, Frank and Morris. Unclear records make it difficult to establish a date for their first automobile. However, the November 21, 1900 issue of *The Horseless Age* carried the following:

"G.H. Eckhart (father of Frank and Morris), candidate for governor of Indiana on the Prohibition Ticket, made his canvass during the recent campaign in an automobile. Mr. Eckhart is a carriage manufacturer and proposes manufacturing automobiles in the near future." Plus, the Auburn Automobile Company extensively used the slogan "Established 1900."

But it wasn't until 1903 that The Auburn Automobile Company was incorporated. The first Auburn automobiles were one-cylinder, solid-tired, tiller-steered, and sold for $800. In 1906, the company leased the former Model Gas Engine Works buildings at the end of Main Street just south of the Vandalia Railroad from the Auburn Commercial Club. The main building currently houses the Auburn Street Department. Auburn was a good solid car and competed well in the era when there were hundreds, if not thousands, of different makes available.

The Eckharts sold the company to a group of Chicago investors headed by William Wrigley, Jr., in 1919. Introduction of the Auburn Beauty-Six in 1919 gave sales a brief boost, only to decline again. By 1924, the company was producing only six units per day, and more than 700 unsold touring cars filled the storage lot.

In an attempt to inject some new life into the company, the Chicago investors hired Errett Lobban Cord as general manager in 1924. Cord had garnered the investors' attention while he was the aggressive sales manager of the Moon Automobile Agency in Chicago. Cord agreed to work for a nominal salary with the understanding that, if he turned the company around, he could acquire a controlling interest.

Upon arriving in Auburn, Cord ordered the stagnant inventory repainted in snappy colors and had trim and accessories added to give them a more engaging look. The inventory was soon liquidated. He then turned around and paid a reputed $50 for a flashy new design in time to put it on the floor of the 1925 New York Auto Show--without getting the company one cent in debt. Sales increased rapidly, and in 1926, Cord became president of the company.

Starting in 1926 Cord conceived his plan to build up a self-sufficient organization, similar to Ford, that could produce practically all the parts needed for automobiles, without having to buy a lot of material outside. He felt he could reduce costs this way. Cord acquired control of Ansted Engine Company, Lexington Motor Car Company, and Central Manufacturing of Connersville; Lycoming Manufacturing Company (and subsidiaries) of Williamsport, Pennsylvania;

Pennsylvania; Limousine Body Company of Kalamazoo, Michigan; and Duesenberg Motors Company of Indianapolis. Growth in Auburn company continued. In five years, E.L. Cord had increased production 1,000 percent. On June 14, 1929 the Cord Corporation was organized with a capitalization of $125 million as a holding company to centralized his growing activities.

In 1928, Alan H. Leamy was hired as a stylist, who introduced the fabulous Auburn boat-tail speedster. Gordon Buehrig designed the Auburn 851, which was introduced in August 1934--one of the first mid-year introductions. Buehrig also designed the Auburn 851 boat-tail speedster with a price tag of $2,100. The speedster is regarded by many as one of the most beautiful cars ever built. Critical acclaim and styling success did not add up to a commercial success. The Depression finally caught up with Auburn in the mid-thirties. The last Auburns were built in 1936.

Here is a list of Auburn production totals:

1924	2,474
1925	4,044
1926	7,138
1927	14,515
1928	12,899
1929	23,509
1930	12,985
1931	34,228
ranking 14th in U.S. retail sales	
1932	11,145
1933	5,038
1934	7,770
1935	6,316
1936	1,263

Cord

The Cord L-29 was introduced in 1929. It was the first production automobile with front wheel drive and was introduced to fill the gap between the low-priced Auburn and the top-of-the-mark Duesenberg in the Cord Corporation line. The sedan and brougham were $3095 each, and the cabriolet and phaeton were $3295 each. Project engineer C.W. Van Ranst designed the new front-wheel drive system around the units in the fabulously successful Harry Miller Indianapolis 500 race cars. The L-29 was built 1929-1932 with only 5,010 produced.

After a lapse of four years the Cord name was revived in July of 1935 with the decision to produce the model 810 in time for the December New York Auto Show introducing the 1936 models. The deadline was made because the cars did not have transmissions, which were still being developed, and the phaetons were all shown with the tops down because these particular cars didn't have any tops. None of this mattered. The Cord 810 stopped the show. People had to stand on surrounding cars just to get a glimpse of Cord's exciting new design. Cord received over 7,600 requests for more information on the 810.

Innovations on the Cord 810 included disappearing headlights, concealed door hinges, rheostat-controlled instrument lights, variable speed windshield wipers, Bendix Electric Hand (steering column mounted--electric gear pre-selection unit) and factory installed radio. The model also was the first automobile in the United States to adopt unit body construction in its full sense. (Chrysler, Airflow, Lincoln, Zepher used modified forms.)

On February 15, 1936, the first Cord 810 rolled off the assembly line in Connersville, with many departments moving to this area within a few months. This decision caused much bitterness in Auburn.

The super-charged Cord 812, which boasted chrome-plated external exhaust pipes and was capable of speeds in excess of 100 mph, was introduced in November 1936. The auto market remained soft in 1937 and production fell to around 1,400 units. Production of the Cord automobile was terminated on October 9, 1937. The Cord automobile and the Cord Corporation died of a common business disease--no profits.

Dallas Winslow, the parts and service man, bought the Auburn showroom and administration building and all the Auburn Cord Duesenberg parts bins. He continued to service and restore these three makes at this location for about twenty years. Today, the building is the setting for the world renowned Auburn Cord Duesenberg Museum.

Other models (in alphabetically order)

Auburn Motor Chassis Company built an inexpensive highwheeler known as the Handy Wagon from 1912-1915. It was one of the last high wheel vehicles manufactured and was popular in rural areas with poor roads. The price was only $487.50 by mail order.

The W.H. Kiblinger Company incorporated in January 1907 with a capitalization of $75,000. The proceeds were used to purchase the plant of the Auburn Wagon and Buggy Works on West Seventh Street. The Kiblinger was a high wheel vehicle that sold for as little as $250, which was extremely reasonable. Within a year, the booming business acquired a building on Lincoln Street between South Wayne and Van Buren streets. In December 1908, via a court decree as a result of a patent suit, the company name was changed to W.H. McIntyre Company.

Early McIntyre models continued to be high wheelers. A few years later the company introduced a truck line up to a five-ton capacity. In 1911, the company purchased the Motor Car Company of America, then located in New York City, and moved it to Auburn. McIntyre wanted to add a large standard car to its line after several years of making high wheel vehicles. The new model was known as the McIntyre Special.

The Imp cycle car was built in 1913-1914 at the rate of about 50 per month in the W.H. McIntyre plant on 500 West Seventh Street (now housing Rieke Corporation). An example of the Imp resides at the Auburn Cord Duesenberg Museum. In its time the company produced the largest range of vehicles of any company in Auburn. In August 1915, the company was forced in bankruptcy.

The Model Gas Engine Works produced the Model automobile in Auburn from 1903 to 1906. A unique feature of the Model was that the entire body of the car was hinged at the rear so that it could be tipped up for access to the under-seat engine and other mechanical parts. This predates today's tilt cab feature on over-the-road trucks. The company moved to Peru in 1906.

In 1915, Auburn Automobile Company acquired Zimmerman Manufacturing Company and organized it as the Union Automobile Company. The Union auto was conceived as a four-cylinder automobile to give more range to the Auburn line, which had only six-cylinder models. The venture was short-lived, lasting one season.

The Zimmerman Manufacturing Company produced a varied line of automobiles from 1907 to 1915. America's first DeSoto was made by Zimmerman between 1913 and 1914. The company also produced some vehicles under lease/contract for the Auburn Automobile. In 1915, production under the Zimmerman name was discontinued, and the plant on North Indiana Avenue was leased to Auburn Automobile Company for the production of the Union automobile.

Current history

Auburn maintains its links with the automobile by supplying a wide range of automotive components including the following manufacturers: Auburn Gear (differentials and gear boxes), Cooper Tire & Rubber (engine mounts), Dana Corporation (clutches) and Guardian Automotive (auto glass).

Roadside Attractions

The Auburn Cord Duesenberg Museum is the only auto museum occupying an original auto factory showroom and administration building. The art-deco structure was built in 1930 for the Auburn Automobile Company and is listed on the National Register of Historic Places. The museum dedicates a large portion to Indiana-built automobiles from the 1890s through 1960s. Other highlights include Packard, Cadillac, Rolls Royce and race cars among its 100-plus automobile collection.
1600 South Wayne Street, 219-925-1444
Hours: daily, 9 a.m. to 5 p.m.; closed Jan. 1, Thanksgiving and Christmas

The buildings now housing the National Automotive and Truck Museum of the United States once contained the production of the L-29 Cord as well as the service facility for the Auburn Automobile Company. NATMUS features trucks from 1907 to the present.
1000 Gordon M. Buehig Place (behind the ACD Museum), 219-925-9100
Hours: daily, 9 a.m. to 5 p.m.; closed Jan. 1, Thanksgiving and Christmas

Columbus

The 1935 Auburn-Cummins, America's first diesel-powered production car, never reached production, although several prototypes were made and demonstrated publicly. This was a joint venture between the Auburn Automobile Company and the Cummins Engine Company.

Cummins is an honored name at the Indianapolis Motor Speedway. In 1931, the company's entry completed the 500 mile race non-stop. In 1952, the Cummins Diesel Special won the coveted pole position and was leading the race before it was eliminated by rubber clogging its supercharger intake.

Today Cummins Engine is the nation's leading manufacturer of over-the-road and off-road diesel engines, turbochargers, and electronics for diesel engines. Arvin Industries also makes automotive stampings and exhaust systems in Columbus.

The Reeves Pulley Company produced two unique automobiles between 1908 and 1912, the Octoauto and the Sextoauto. Early Reeves autos were highwheelers with air-cooled engines, but in 1911 the Octoauto was introduced. The Octoauto had two axles each at front and rear, six of the eight wheels were steerable and a 175-inch wheelbase. The main advertising claim for the Octoauto was its increased comfort provided by the eight-wheels. The Sextoauto introduced in 1912 had two wheels in front and four wheels in the rear.

Today Reeves is a division of Reliance Electric and produces motor drives, transmissions and pulleys.

Did you know?

There are several racing events happening throughout the state. Call the following for track information.

Bunker Hill–Drag Strip	765-689-8248
Haubstadt–Tri-State Speedway	821-768-5995
Jeffersonville–Sportsdrome Speedway	812-282-7551
Medaryville–Shady Hill Raceway	219-843-8892
Paragon–Speedway	765-537-2366
Plymouth–Capitol Speedway	219-935-4414

Roadside attractions

(Columbus-Bedford-Bloomington-Seymour area)
The Antique Auto and Race Car Museum in Bedford features about 100
notable race, classic and special interest cars.
off U.S. 37 at the intersection of Highway 50, 812-275-0556
Hours: April through December, Monday through Saturday,
noon to 8 p.m.

The Bloomington Speedway is one of Indiana's best dirt oval tracks,
established in 1923. Visitors can see midget, sprint and stock car racing every
other weekend from mid-April to late-September.
5185 Fairfax Road, 812-824-7400 (call for a schedule)

The automobile was a natural offspring of the buggy. A building that once
included Studebaker buggy assembly is now a bed and breakfast inn called
The Story Inn in Nashville.
6404 State Road 135 South, 812-988-2273

Al's Heartbeat Cafe in Seymour doubles as a restaurant and museum. The
diner has a 1950's retro-look with the museum displaying a few cars and
trucks from the era.
1541 W. Tipton (U.S. 50 W), 812-522-4574
Hours: Sunday through Thursday, 11 a.m. to 9 p.m.; Friday and Saturday,
11 a.m. to 10 p.m.

Connersville

The Automobile Manufacturers Association lists ten models that
can be called Connersville-made cars. Listed chronologically they are
Central (1905), McFarlan (1909-1928), Lexington (1910-1926), Empire (1912-1915), Kelsey Cycle Car (1913-1914), Lexington-Howard
(1914), Van Auken Electric (1914), Ansted (1927), Auburn (1929-
1937) and Cord (1936-1937). During the 32 years from the first to
the last models, the Connersville community was very much alive as
automotive center in the United States. One journalist nicknamed
the town the "Little Detroit of Indiana."

Connersville made the move to the automotive age in 1886 when
John B. McFarlan converted part of the family farm into one of the
first industrial parks in the country. In his desire to expand his

carriage business, he lit the spark for what turned out to be a center for automobile production and automotive component manufacturing, which exists today. Most of the auto production buildings in the McFarlan industrial park also remain.

Central Manufacturing Company was incorporated on April 7, 1898 to manufacture vehicle woodwork at 123 West Seventh Street, on the site now occupied by Val Discount store. In 1903, it began to manufacture rear-entrance automobile bodies for Cadillac. A Central car was built in this plant in 1905, but unfortunately the car was lost when the plant burned in 1905. The company moved to a new building in McFarlan's park (on 18th Street north of the intersection at Georgia Street) in 1906. Central bodies became standard units on Stutz, National, Premier, Cole, H.C.S., Moon, Gardner, Wescott, Davis, Auburn, Elcar, Haynes, Apperson, Paige, Overland, Lexington, and Empire automobiles.

The McFarlan auto was the outgrowth of the McFarlan Carriage Company (on the south end of the industrial park), which turned to manufacturing automobiles in 1909. The company produced automobiles built to customer specifications for the next 19 years. A 1923 McFarlan Knickerbocker Cabriolet priced at $25,000, complete with all gold-plated outside trim, was shown at the National Automobile Show in Chicago.

In 1910, a group of Connersville businessmen noted that the community had too much tied up in the buggy and carriage industry, which was being displaced by the growing use of the automobile. The group enticed the infant Lexington Motor Car Company to relocate from Lexington, Kentucky to a new plant at 800 West 18th Street in the industrial park. The company was promotion-minded and entered both the Glidden Tour and the Indianapolis 500 in 1912. Financial difficulties were solved in 1913 when the Ansted family acquired Lexington. In 1914, the new Lexington-Howard Company produced the Howard automobile. In 1915, the named changed back to Lexington Motor Company. With the new Ansted engine, Lexington cars became modern and powerful. Two short-wheelbase race cars with the powerful Ansted engine were built by Lexington for the 1920 Pikes Peak hill climb. The driver won that race and the 1924 event. The Penrose trophy, given to the driver for his 1924 victory, is on display at the Reynolds Museum on Vine Street.

The formation of the United States Automotive Corporation was announced by President Frank B. Ansted on January 12, 1920. It was a $10 million merger with the Lexington Motor Car Company, the Ansted Engineering Company, The Connersville Foundry Corporation and the Teetor-Harley Motor Corporation of Hagerstown. On December 16, 1921, William C. Durant, founder of General Motors and former GM president, ordered 30,000 Ansted engines for his new Durant Six that was being built in Muncie by Durant Motors, Inc. Central Manufacturing built bodies for the Durant automobile.

The Lexington star descended about as rapidly as it had ascended. On May 10, 1927, E.L. Cord purchased Lexington Motor Car Company and Ansted Engineering.

In 1912, Indianapolis businessmen Carl G. Fisher and Charles Sommers decided to contract for all parts and final assembly of their Empire Automobile by Rex Wheel Works (between Lexington Motor Car and Central Manufacturing in the industrial park on 18th Street). Central Manufacturing received the contract for the bodies, and the Rex Manufacturing Company made the tops and enclosures. Teetor-Harley engines were used during the seven-year contract with Empire. In 1919, The Greenville Car Company of Greenville, Pennsylvania, bought the Empire name and designs.

The Connersville Buggy Company built prototypes of the Kelsey Cycle Car about 1913. But, the cycle-car fad ended in 1914 before they reached production. Their next venture in 1914 was a parcel post van, built under contract for Van Auken Electric Company of Chicago. Electric vehicles were not too practical at this time, and the contract was short-lived.

At the time that Cord was putting together his plan for a self-sufficient organization, a committee of Connersville officials asked him to look over the idle Lexington Motor Car Company and the adjacent Ansted Engineering buildings. In 1927, Cord purchased these facilities. In 1928, he purchased the Central Manufacturing Company (directly east of his previous two purchases) and added 110,000 square feet more manufacturing space to the existing Central facilities. Cord bought the McFarlan Motor Car plant five blocks south of his existing plants in 1929.

Cord then invested $2 million in plant and production facilities. The new manufacturing plant was comparable to the most modern assembly plants anywhere in the world. It consisted of 20 buildings on 82 acres, and 1,500,000 square feet of manufacturing area available for the production of 400 bodies and 250 completed cars per day. The operation may have been a predecessor to "Just-In-Time" manufacturing, a concept of having the right materials at the right time attributed to recent decades. Sheet metal, wood, engines and other materials entered the plant on the northeast side, and the completed car was delivered to the customer near the southwest corner. On January 15, 1929, the first Auburn 6-80 sedan, rolled off the 900-foot final assembly line. Seventy-five percent of Auburn's cars were built in Connersville until 1933. In the fall of 1933, Cord moved the Limousine Body Company of Kalamazoo, Michigan (builder of the Auburn open car bodies) into the Central Manufacturing facilities. By 1934, all Auburn final production was done at the 82-acre Connersville center.

In August 1935, several employees on the Auburn line were relocated near the final assembly area. It was announced that the revolutionary new 1936 Cord model 810 would be built in there. On February 15, 1936, the first production model 810 rolled off the final assembly line. (See the Cord discussion in the Auburn section for more detail on the model 810.) In May 1936, executive, administrative, engineering and production departments were moved to Connersville. All production efforts were put behind the 1937 Cord model 812, but production only totaled about 1,300 units. E.L.Cord announced on August 7, 1937, that the Cord Corporation had been sold to the Aviation Corporation headed by Victor Emanuel. About 3,000 cars were built in the two-year run of the model 810/812, ending the Auburn/Cord production. Yet, the legacy continues as nearly two-thirds of these cars have been restored by auto buffs around the world.

The non-automotive stamping business of the Cord Corporation had been profitable since its inception in the early thirties.

In 1938, however, the Auburn Automobile Company announced that it had purchased the Pak-Age-Car Division from Stutz in Indianapolis. Auburn would produce the multi-stop delivery truck until 1941. Howard Darrin was allowed to build his Packard Darrin in the factory during 1940 and 1941. On March 10, 1941, Willys-Overland awarded Auburn-Central (the new corporate name) a contract to to build 1,600 Jeep bodies. This was the first of many contracts that lasted through 1948 for Willys and Ford. The total for Jeep bodies reached 445,000 over a 45-month period.

Today automotive component production still exists in or near McFarlan's industrial park through the Stant company at 1620 Columbia Avenue (radiator caps, oil breather caps, locking gas caps, and pressure cap testers), and Ford Electronics and Refrigeration just north on State Route 1 (automotive air conditioners & components).

Roadside attractions

The Reynolds Museum offers a look at the history of the area, including a view of how the automobile industry influenced the town, and houses the trophy won by a Connersville-made car, the Lexington, for the 1924 Pikes Peak hill climb.
corner of Howard and Vine (St. Rd. 1 S.) streets,
765-825-5325 (curator's number)
Hours: March through November, Sundays, 2 to 5 p.m.
call for appointment

The homes of auto pioneers J. B. McFarland and Frank B. Ansted still stand and have been beautifully maintained and renovated. Now private residences, the MacFarland house is at the corner of 8th and Lincoln streets, and the Ansted house is at 1205 N. Central.

Elkhart

Elkhart produced cars, taxicabs, and trucks from 1906 to 1934. In sheer numbers of auto manufacturers, only Indianapolis rivaled Elkhart in Indiana. Like many of the U.S. automobile producers, the Elkhart companies were assemblers and body builders.

None of the local companies produced a complete product from raw materials as did the major companies such as Ford, General Motors, Chrysler, and Studebaker. Design and styling of the Elkhart-produced cars were usually dependent on the need to use components purchased from outside suppliers and limited production facilities. Competition from the larger manufacturers and the small profits common among assemblers forced the Elkhart companies out of the market.

The drama begins with the Elkhart Carriage and Harness Manufacturing Company whose predecessor was started in 1873 to produce buggies and carriages. Elkhart Carriage sold everything through mail order. In 1906, the Pratt brothers, the Elkhart Carriage founders, developed their first experimental model. In 1909, they began manufacturing the Pratt-Elkhart, described as "a standard automobile along modern lines." They were not successful selling their car through mail order, so they began advertising for dealers. At this time they dropped the "Elkhart" from the name.

In 1916, the corporate name changed to Elkhart Carriage and Motor Car Company and the trade name of the Pratt to Elcar. The Pratt had a price of around $2,000, a little steep in those days. The Elcar came in at the low price of $795. Elcar's slogan was "The Car for the Many." As a result of World War I, the company ceased its automobile and carriage production in 1918 and made ambulance bodies for the army. Automobile production resumed in 1919, and by 1922 ten models of pleasure cars were being produced.

On July 1, 1922, the Pratt brothers retired and sold the company to a group of executives from the Auburn Automobile Company. At the same time, the corporate name changed to Elcar Motor Company. In late 1922, Elcar entered the taxicab market. The company produced cabs under many names including ElFay, Martel, Paragon, and Royal Martel.

By the late 1920s and the early 1930s, Elcar was beginning to feel the financial pinch and, as a final attempt to compete, purchased the Mercer name from the defunct Mercer Company of New Jersey. Only two Mercers were produced. Elcar Motor Company ceased operations in 1932.

In 1933, the Elcar plant (the Riverside plant was on West Beardsley) was taken over by Allied Products Manufacturing Company owned by Jules Martin. Allied Cab Company was the new venture to produce taxis from 1932 to 1934. The company produced three lines: Allied, Super Allied, and Prosperity Cab.

Dr. E.C. Crow and his son Martin E. Crow started Crow Motor Car Company in 1909. The factory was located in buildings on North Main St. (Excel Industries, manufacturers of truck parts & accessories, now occupies 1120 N. Main.) Crow produced autos for direct resale under the Black Crow, Crow, and Crow Elkhart names.

Crow also was a contract manufacturer for companies like Birch, Bush, Bush Temple, and Mutual Motor Car Company. These companies would sell the car by mail order and get the money up front. Crow would then manufacture the car and sell it wholesale. Crow fit this role especially well due to its production capacity.

In 1919 the Crow Company sold its interests to a group of New York and Ohio capitalists. In 1920, 5,000 cars were produced. On January 26, 1921, control of Crow Elkhart Motor Corporation passed into the hands of an eastern syndicate headed by the Discount Company of Massachusetts. From 1919 to 1924 Crow also had an export subsidiary known as Century Motor Company, which assembled the Morris-London for export to England.

Morris-Londons were available as touring cars or landaulets and later designed for use as taxis. In 1925 the Morris-London was built by Century Motor Company, an offshoot of the mother company in an attempt to preserve this contract. This plan failed, as did both companies in 1925.

The Elkhart Motor Car Company started producing two models in the medium price range, the Sterling and the Komet in 1911 in the Sterling Avenue plant. The Sterling was built in five body styles, ranging from $1,500 to $1,850. The plant and assets were sold to a group of former Haynes Auto Company executives in 1911. They formed the Elmer Automobile Company. The group bought Elkhart Motor Car Company to speed up production. The Elmer and the Lohr models saw only prototype production before Elkhart Motor Car Company creditors filed suit. The Elmer Group found investors in Cleveland, Ohio, and later moved production there.

In 1915 the Sterling Company was sold to the Sun Motor Company of Buffalo, New York. Sun produced cars for a year at the Sterling plant, and in 1916 sold the plant to the Huffman Brothers Motor Company. Sun moved to a smaller plant at the corner of Richmond and MacDonald streets. At this location they continued to produce a small, low-priced, six-cylinder touring car rated at 22 hp. The plant closed in 1918.

The Huffman Brothers Motor Company began in late 1919 in the Sterling Avenue factory on Sterling Avenue, purchased from Sun
continued on page 20

Behind the wheel

The Izzers were made for a wealthy Chicago industrialist in 1912. The automobile received its name because the owner didn't want a "was-er" or a "has-been." Only three Izzers were made. And one of the Izzers still is—on display in the Auburn Cord Duesenberg Museum in Auburn.

* * * * * *

Mrs. Mary Landon, a stenographer for Haynes-Apperson, became the first woman in America to drive a gasoline-powered automobile.

* * * * * *

The Greater Crown Point Chamber of Commerce sponsors a historical reenactment of The Cobe Cup rally. The 23-mile race commemorates one of the original road races founded early in automotive history. The Cobe Cup was the name of the trophy given to the winner of the original race held in 1909. This 410-mile race predates the Indianapolis 500 by two years. Current races allow only pre-1979 era cars, trucks and motorcycles.

* * * * * *

In 1908, the Joseph J. Cole entered the newly established field of automobile manufacturing in Indianapolis. He was so excited about the prospect of driving his first automobile that he forgot that one important accessory was missing—the brakes. He spent most of the afternoon on this initial test run driving around and around Monument Circle in downtown until the car ran out of gas, providing the necessary means to stop the car.

* * * * * *

During the 1950s, several years after selling the Cord Corporation, E.L. Cord served as a state senator representing Nevada.

Motor Company the previous year. By 1920 Huffman ranked sixth in the United States as a producer of quality trucks. The Huffman truck was like other "assembled" automobiles and trucks produced at that time. All parts other than the frame, small chassis parts, and body panels were bought from other companies. Huffman also made a typical assembled car in both open and closed models, beginning in 1920. Huffmans were sold mainly in the Midwest. About 3,000 units were made. The company only produced cars and trucks to order. Production of Huffman cars and trucks ended in 1925.

During this time in Elkhart, a number of other cars, trucks, taxis and other specialized vehicles were assembled in Elkhart. Many of these were produced by companies that left little trace of their existence.

Today Elkhart is a large producer of mobile homes and recreational vehicles. Other automotive products include vehicular lighting, electrical equipment for internal combustion engines, truck & bus bodies, truck parts & accessories, and van conversions. A large portion of van conversions and recreational vehicles in the midwest come from the Elkhart-Goshen area.

Roadside attractions

The Recreational Vehicle and Motor Home Hall of Fame celebrates industry pioneers. The museum features restored trailers dating from 1928.
801 Benham Avenue, 219-293-2344
Hours: Monday through Friday, 9 a.m. to 4 p.m.
weekends by appointment

The S. Ray Miller Antique Auto Museum displays about 40 rare and prize-winning show cars, including a 1930 Duesenberg and several Studebaker models, surrounded by memorabilia reflecting automotive history.
2130 Middlebury Street, 219-522-0539
Hours: Monday through Friday, 10 p.m. to 4 p.m.
last complete weekend of each month, noon to 4 p.m.

Ruthmere Museum is the refurbished home of A. R. Beardsley, one of the founders of Miles Laboratories. The house combines elaborate French Beaux Arts style with functional Prairie School architecture. On display in the garage are three antique cars, a 1912 Pratt (made in Elkhart), a 1916 Milburn Electric and a 1917 Cadillac.

302 E. Beardsley Avenue, 219-264-0330

Hours for guided tours: Tuesday through Saturday, 11 a.m., 1 and 3 p.m. (in July and August) 3 p.m. on Sunday

closed Dec. 15 through Mar. 31, Memorial Day, July 4 and Thanksgiving

In nearby Shipshewana, Dad's Toys sells collectible toy cars, trucks, farm vehicles and semi-trucks. The business also provides mail-order services.

SR 5 and Middlebury Street, 800-645-4725

Hours: Monday through Saturday, 9 a.m. to 7 p.m. (closes at 5 p.m. during winter months)

Evansville

The Single-Center Buggy Company made the Single-Center motor buggy (1906-1908) with a 159 c.i., two-cylinder water-cooled engine. It was available with either solid rubber or pneumatic tires.

The Traveler was manufactured by the Traveler Motor Car Company between 1910 and 1911. Traveler models were a two-passenger runabout and a five-passenger touring car with 30-hp and 35-hp four-cylinder engines respectively. Both models had selective three-speed transmissions.

The Evansville Automobile Company made two autos, the Simplicity (1907-1911) and the Evansville (1907-1909) The Simplicity offered touring cars, roadsters and limousines with four-cylinder, water-cooled engines and dual-disc transmissions. This transmission was advertised as giving "all the speeds of a locomotive without a gear." The Evansville was available with either a 20-hp or a 30-hp engine and a three-speed selective gear transmission. The Simplicity introduced the first honeycomb radiator for automobiles.

The Graham Brothers Truck plant was built in 1919. Dodge engines and other components were used in a variety of Graham trucks. When the firm merged with Dodge in 1925, the brothers became Dodge executives. Dodge merged with Chrysler Corporation in 1928. In 1935, Chrysler converted the Dodge truck plant over for assembly of the Plymouth. Plymouths were produced there until 1956, ending Evansville's link to automobile production.

continued on page 23

Behind the wheel

The Lincoln Highway was inaugurated in 1913, at a time when 180,000 cars were registered in a nation of 2.5 million miles of mostly dirt roads. Few people had knowledge of roads beyond a 15-mile radius, and road maps and signs were nearly nonexistent west of Chicago, Illinois.

During this time, U.S. automobile owners could obtain an essential factor for traveling–the vehicle. They needed the other part of the equation–decent roads. One person realizing the American public's yen for on-the-road adventures was an Indianapolis entrepreneur and one of the founders of the Indianapolis Motor Speedway, Carl Fisher. Although he wasn't the first to visualize a transcontinental highway, he was the first to determine a feasible plan to finance the vision. In September 1912, he decided to get pledges from automobile and accessories manufacturers. The contributors were motivated by the idea that if there were decent roads, people would travel more and product demand would increase. Within 30 days he had $1 million in pledges and publicity nationwide. It was enough to start the process.

Fisher and others playing a prominent role in the highway, which was dedicated to the memory of President Abraham Lincoln, still had to contend mostly with a dirt road. Their efforts, however, enlighted large and small communities on the advantages of well-maintained roads and highways. In fact, every community wanted its own national highway. "New roads began to spring up like weeds in an untended garden," writes Drake Hokanson in the 1988 book *The Lincoln Highway: Main Street Across America.* This led the federal government to adopt a numbered highway system in 1925. "The new federal highway system was a near fatal blow to the Lincoln Highway and a death knell for all the other named highways of the country."

Yet, one of the goals of the Lincoln Highway founders had been realized. The nation became linked through a network of hard-surfaced, all-weather roads.

The present-day route loosely follows U.S. 30 from Ohio to Fort Wayne; U.S. 33 north to Ligonier, Goshen and South Bend; then U.S. 20 west to near Rolling Prairie where it merges with S.R. 2; follow S.R. 2 to Laporte and Valparaiso; then U.S. 30 through Dyer.

The story of the Graham brothers, however, doesn't end yet. They were too energetic to work for others, and in 1927 they bought out the Paige-Detroit auto firm. Evansville's citizenry was excited by the prospects at the new Graham-Paige auto plant in 1929. The 1932 Graham introduced the use of full-skirted fenders. Their euphoria was soon squelched by the Great Depression's pall. After the plant closed, only the Detroit plant made Graham cars until 1941.

The Muntz Jet was produced by the Muntz Car Company at Evansville in 1950 and 1951. The Muntz Jet represented the commercial production of its predecessor Kurtis Sports that had been designed and built by Frank Kurtis. He enjoyed a successful career building race cars, many of which were successful at the Indianapolis Motor Speedway. The Evansville works built this racy two-door convertible with a 329 c.i., 133 hp, Cadillac V-8 engine.

Fort Wayne

Fort Wayne's link to automotive history occurred in 1885 when Sylvanus F. Bowser of Fort Wayne invented the world's first gas pump. International Harvester made the scene in 1923 when it opened its truck plant. This plant closed in 1983 after the 1,527,299th truck rolled off the line. This facility also produced the Scout from 1961-1980.

In 1986, the General Motors Truck & Bus Group opened an assembly plant in Roanoke, (a suburb of Fort Wayne) which is one of GM's most efficient plants. They produce a truck a minute, mostly sport utility vehicles.

Fort Wayne is also the headquarters for Tokheim Corporation, one of the world's largest producers of gasoline pumps and service station dispensing equipment.

Roadside attractions

The Fort Wayne Firefighters Museum is a converted firehouse built in 1893. On display are seven antique fire trucks and an ambulance.
226 W. Washington Street, 219-426-0051
Wed. only, 10 a.m. to 8 p.m.

Cindy's Diner is an original 1950s diner restored to accommodate 15 patrons at a time.
830 S. Harrison Street, 219-422-1957
Hours: Monday through Friday, 6 a.m. to 8 p.m.
Saturday and Sunday, 7 a.m. to 2 p.m.

Indianapolis

Indianapolis was a commercial producer of automobiles and taxicabs from 1896 to 1937. The Circle City with 65 different vehicles manufactured here ranked second to Cleveland, with 82, as Detroit's chief rival for the title of the nation's auto capital. David L. Lewis notes in *The Automobile in American Culture* that until 1905 Indianapolis contained more auto plants than did any city in Michigan.

Indianapolis makes, such as Duesenberg, Marmon, and Stutz, are highly sought after by collectors today and have achieved the "Classic" designation from the Classic Car Club of America. The Indianapolis Motor Speedway built in 1909 was the birthplace for many engineering improvements and played an important part in the development process for Indianapolis makers as well as other autos. As with the majority of manufacturers around the state, the companies in Indianapolis were primarily assemblers. They concentrated on providing uniqueness to their products, which also proved to be their undoing. They were not able to compete with the mass producers who could control all components of the process and, therefore, offer a product at a much lower price. Today we can only enjoy their handy work at museums or collector-car meets.

The following lists, in chronological order, most of the auto companies making Indianapolis history:

Black

Charles H. Black, the proprietor of a local carriage and blacksmith shop (44 S. Pennsylvania, currently the Century Building, c 1900), got the urge to construct a horseless carriage after driving a neighbor's imported Benz in 1891. (*See sidebar about this journey.*) He claims to have constructed an automobile of his own design similar to the Benz sometime in 1893. Unfortunately, no contemporary newspaper or magazine accounts exist to corroborate his claimed date. Commercial production of the Black by C.H. Black Manufacturing Co.

occurred from 1896 to 1900. At some point he printed a catalog describing five models from the lightweight two-passenger auto to a 10-passenger wagon, priced at $1800. It is believed that most of his cars were sold locally. In 1899 he named the company the Indianapolis Automobile and Vehicle Company, and the autos were named Indianapolis. In 1900, Black sold his design and rights to a group of local businessmen who produced the Black as the Indiana in 1901.

Waverly

The original Waverly electric made by Waverly Company from (1898-1903) was a two-passenger car with tiller steering and a single headlight that sold for $850. The company was reorganized as the International Motor Car Company (1901-1903) and PopeWaverly (1904-1908). During the Pope regime the line of models was expanded to include more bodies, plus a miniature limousine with a wheelbase of only 90 in. After the failure of Pope again under Waverly Company (1908-1914), a large range of cars was marketed, with four different shaft drive models in 1914, similar in appearance to gasoline cars.

National

The National Automobile & Electric Company was founded by L.S. Dow and Phillip Goetz in 1900. The first National vehicles were light, electric runabouts. In 1904 the company was reorganized as the National Motor Vehicle Company. By 1905, a gasoline auto was developed with a four-cylinder Rutenber engine. Electric cars were dropped in 1906. National introduced a six-cylinder model in 1906, one of the first in America. Its cylinders were cast separately until 1908, when engines with paircast cylinders and a U.S. shield-shaped radiator design were introduced.

During this period, racing played an important part in National's plans. National finished seventh in the Inaugural 500 Mile Race on Memorial Day, 1911. Additional 1911 competition road race victories include Elgin Illinois, Santa Monica, and the Cactus Derby from Los Angeles to Phoenix. A National won the Indianapolis 500 Mile Race in 1912 with an average speed of 78.7 mph.

In 1912 the company focused on production of a variety of fours and sixes with pricing starting at $2,500. Five models were available in the 1914 line with prices ranging from $2,750 to $3,400 each.

continued on page 27

Behind the wheel

The monuments of several notable automobile pioneers and notable figures are in Crown Hill Cemetary, 700 W. 38th Street, Indianapolis. The following shows the location of monuments with the section number listed first and then the lot number.

Automobile manufacturers:
C.H. Black (Charles) 25, 185
Frederick Duesenberg, 104, 294
August Duesenberg, Community Mausoleum, D-2-MM
Harry C. Stutz, 47, 334
Marmon, Walter C., 29, 44; Howard C. 29, 44; Franklin H. 29, 44; Daniel W. co-founder 29, 44.

Founders of the Indianapolis 500
James A. Allison, 23, 2
Carl G. Fisher, 13, 42
Ronald Fisher, 62, 719
Arthur C. Newby, 23, 39
Frank H. Wheeler, 46, 24

Race car drivers
George Amick, 235, 723
Edwin Cannonball Baker, 60, 150
Floyd E. Davis, 53, 320
Ronnie Duman, 224, 106
Frank P. Fox, 104, 293
Gerald P. Hoyt, 223-53
Jim Hurtuibise, mausoleum D-8-2DD
C.J. Chet Miller, Mausoleum A-B-19
Paul Rousso, 78, 83
Louis Schneider, 42, 124
Louis Schwitzer, 61, 3 mausoleum
Howard Wilcox, 56, 240

For help in locating grave stones, contact the Crown Hill office, Monday through Friday, 8:30 a.m. to 5 p.m., and Saturday, 8:30 a.m. and 2 p.m. On Sunday, you can find information at the community mausoleum, 9 a.m. to 5 p.m.

In 1915 a new range of models were announced with a six or the National Highway 12 in the same chassis. The 12 was dropped in 1920, and National soldiered on with six-cylinder cars for the last four years. A merger in 1922 between National, Dixie Flyer and Jackson led to a range of three cars for 1923 and 1924. In January 1924 the company moved into receivership.

Marmon

Howard C. Marmon's first prototype car for Nordyke and Marmon Company was remarkably progressive for 1902. It featured an overhead valve, air-cooled, two-cylinder, 90-degree V configuration engine with pressure lubrication. It was the earliest automotive application of a system that had long since become universal to internal combustion piston engine design. Howard Marmon's first cars were advanced machines, featuring air-cooled V4 engines with mechanically operated overhead valves and pressure lubrication. His early automobiles employed a separate sub-frame for engine and transmission, an early attempt at independent front suspension. In 1909 Marmon converted to water cooled, conventional T-head, inline four-cylinder engines.

In 1911 Marmon introduced the six-cylinder Model 32 with rear-axle transmission. Ray Harroun won the first Indianapolis 500 Mile Race in 1911 with a racing variation named the Marmon Wasp.

In 1916 the advanced ohv, six-cylinder Model 34 was introduced with aluminum cylinder block, most engine components (including pushrods), body, hood and radiator shell. Developments of this model continued as late as 1927, acquiring Delco coil ignition in 1920 and the option of front wheel brakes in 1923.

In 1926, the firm was reorganized as Marmon Motor Car Company. In 1928 two eight-cylinder models were offered, the cheapest L-head Model 68 selling for $1,395. The company sold 22,300 cars in 1929 because of a low-priced new straight-eight called the Roosevelt. The 1929 Roosevelt had the distinction of being the first eight-cylinder car in the world to sell for less than $1,000. The Roosevelt appeared in the 1930 catalog as the Marmon Roosevelt and only lasted one more year. The 1929 Marmon warrants a listing in the Guiness Book of Records for factory installed radio.

Marmon left the auto business just as it came in with a magnificent 491 c.i., 200-hp, Marmon V-16 in 1931. The eight exceptional body styles were by Walter Dorwin Teague. The Marmon V-16 became the largest American passenger car engine of its era. In February 1931, before production started, the Society of Automotive Engineers honored Colonel Marmon for "the most notable engineering achievement of 1930," his huge and gleaming V-16 engine design. The society was especially impressed by his extensive use of lightweight aluminum, generally a difficult metal to work and maintain in automobile power plants. There was a companion eight-cylinder auto in 1932 but only the 16 was listed for 1933. At the very end, Howard Marmon built, at his own expense, a prototype auto with 150 hp V12 engine, independent front-suspension, DeDion rear axle and tubular backbone frame, with styling by Teague. This model, however, never saw production.

The original Nordyke and Marmon Plant 1 was at the southwest corner of Kentucky Avenue and West Morris Street. Plant 2 was at the southwest corner of Drover and West York Street. Plant 3 was a five-story structure measuring 80 x 600 feet parallel to Morris Street (now Eli Lilly & Company building 314). The Marmon assembly plant was built adjacent to the Morris Street property line with Plant 3 behind and parallel to it (also part of the Eli Lilly complex).

Mohawk

The Mohawk by the Mohawk Auto & Cycle Company (1903-1905) was made as a two- or five-passenger car with single and two-cylinder engines, yielding 7 hp and 18 hp respectively. The smaller car was steered by tiller, while the larger used a steering wheel. Both had wire wheels and pneumatic tires.

Premier

George B. Weidley and Harold O. Smith organized the Premier Motor Manufacturing Company in 1903 with a capitalization of $50,000 for the production of air-cooled cars. Premier claimed that the oak leaf on its radiator badge was the first use of an emblem as an automobile trademark. Premier made the transition to all water-cooled engines in 1908. When Premier completed the 1910 Glidden Tour, it had established an unprecedented record of three perfect scores. The company introduced its first six in 1908, and from 1913 on, only sixes were built. On October 15, 1914, Premier went into receivership. In December 1915, the company was reorganized as the Premier Motor Car Company. The touring Premier of 1918-1920 was notable mainly for its use of the Cutler Hammer Magnetic Gear Shift, an electric transmission system controlled by a push button arrangement mounted on the steering column. The ohv 295 c.i. engine was an unusually advanced six, with a one-piece aluminum block, crankcase and pistons, with cast-iron cylinder liners. In 1920 L.S. Skelton reorganized the company as the Premier Motor Corporation. In the spring of 1923 the company emerged from another receivership as Premier Motors, Inc. In 1923, Premier obtained control of the Monroe Motor Company and then marketed the Monroe four briefly in a redesigned model that included a flat, squared radiator in place of the earlier rounded type. Few were built, and the final cars were marketed as the Premier Model B. Late in 1923 the company received a contract for building 1,000 Premier taxicabs. From then on, taxicabs were the firm's only products. In October 1926, Premier sold out to the National Cab & Truck Company of Indianapolis.

Marion

The Marion Motor Car Company built the Marion from 1904 to 1914. Early versions of the Marion had 16-hp Reeves air-cooled four-cylinder engines. George Schebler of the Wheeler Schebler Carburetor Company used a Marion chassis to build a V-12 roadster in 1908. The 1913 Marion Bobcat roadster was the company's best known sporting car. Throughout its life the Marion Motor Car Company struggled due to low capitalization. In November 1914, J.I. Handley purchased the assets of Marion and moved the operations to Jackson, Michigan.

Overland

Demand for Overland automobiles increased to the point that it was difficult to produce the necessary quantity at the Standard Wheel Works facility in Terre Haute. In 1905 Overland operations were moved to Indianapolis at 900-1300 West Henry Street. In 1906 Claude E. Cox was the president of the Overland Auto Company when Standard Wheel Works sold the car and rights to Parry Manufacturing Company of Indianapolis.

continued on page 31

Behind the wheel

C.H. Black of Indianapolis was one of the early pioneers of automotive history. He probably was one of the first Americans to actually a drive an automobile, a German-made Benz in 1891.

That historic journey in Indianapolis also resulted with another automotive first according to an account related by Black's mechanic. During this six-block drive, Black crashed into a surrey when the horses became frightened–the first automobile accident. At the next turn, the car drove into the Occidental Hotel show window, thereby, creating the second automobile accident. The third happened when the auto destroyed another show window a few feet away.

Acting in accordance with suggestions from the police, Black and his passengers drove back to his carriage factory, ending one of the first automobile journeys in America.

* * * * * *

A story about Carl Fisher, one of the founders of the Indianapolis 500 and the Lincoln Highway, illustrates the lack of adequate facilities for traveling any distance in the early days of the automobile. Around 1912, Fisher and a few friends were driving in unfamiliar territory nine miles outside the city limits of Indianapolis. Night fell along with a torrent of rain. In an open-top car, Fisher and his friends were drenched in seconds and miserably lost. There were no street lights to guide them in the pitch-black night nor road signs marking the way.

They did, however, feel comfortable that they had guessed the way back home until they came to a three-way fork in the road. No one could be sure which fork to take, but someone thought he saw a sign at the top of a pole. Fisher lost the competition as to who would have to climb the pole to read the sign. So he shinnied up the pole and lit a match so that he could read the sign. One match after another was extinguished by rain. Finally one lit so that Fisher could read the sign–"Chew Battle-Ax Plug."

The experience may have been one reason that Fisher became one of the automotive pioneers in making night travel and long-distance drives a reality. Fisher was instrumental in developing head lights and building modern highway systems.

Shortly before the national panic of 1907, John North Willys made a contract with Overland to manufacture 500 cars in 1908, and paid $10,000 to bind the agreement and give the factory the financial ability to increase its facilities. During the panic Overland noted that it could not fill its contract and could not meet its current payroll. Over a weekend, Willys raised the $350 and deposited it to the credit of the Overland Company.

Bankruptcy was stalled for the moment on the pledge that the company would be reorganized with Willys as president, treasurer, general manager, sales manager, and purchasing agent. Overland resumed production. Willys sold 465 cars in that year, paid the most pressing debts, and showed a profit of $58,000. With the inevitable improvement in credit and the available cash, in 1909 he took over the plant of the Pope auto manufacturing facilities in Toledo, Ohio, and started production of a new automobile that he named the Willys-Overland.

American Motors

The product of the American Motors Company is most familiarly known today as the American Underslung, (1906-1914) although this description was seldom used then, the company preferring to go with varying model designations, such as American Scout, American Tourist, American Traveler, and American Roadster. This make achieved its fame from the underslung models, so named because the frame hung below the axles. This gave a low appearance and center of gravity, but didn't sacrifice good ground clearance. This design was introduced in 1907; earlier cars had conventional chassis.

Models in 1908 used 40 and 50 hp, four-cylinder Teetor-Hartley engines. The most rakish models were the roadsters, originally only a two-passenger, but supplemented in 1909 by a long-wheelbase four-passenger. A 70 hp, six-cylinder engine came in 1910.

Cole

The Cole was produced by the Cole Motor Car Company from 1909 to 1925. *(The Cole buildings are at 750 E. Washington Street --remodeled in 1997 for Indianapolis/Marion County Jail Annex and the building immediately behind it on Ohio Street. Above the door it still says Cole Motor Car Company.)* The first Cole, possibly a reflection of the predecessor company's history of horse-drawn carriage manufacturing, was a primitive highwheeler with solid tires, powered by a 14 hp, air-cooled, flat twin engine that was marketed in 1909. It was soon dropped in favor of the Cole 30 with large, conventional fours. A Cole six followed, and in 1913, so did electric lighting and starting. Cole initially eschewed annual model changes, but soon adopted the industry practice. In 1915, one year after Cadillac, Cole introduced its V8 model and soon dropped fours and sixes altogether. Like the majority of Indiana cars, Cole was an assembled car. (Its V-8 came from General Motors' Northway Division, which also built Cadillac's.)

Joseph J. Cole believed that a supplier who was a specialist in only one or a few parts could do a better job than a major manufacturer trying to be a jack-of-all-trades in making all his own parts. Cole adopted the phrase "The Standardized Car" for his product, indicating the use of components that were the standard for quality in the industry. With cars like Cadillac as its peers, Cole never changed his sights to other price fields. The Aero-Eight became the car for which Cole is best remembered. It's the car that, for a brief period, was second only to Cadillac in volume of sales in its price range. The body of the car was light and the lines handsome, and had names like Tourosine, Tuxedo, Sportosine and Ultra-Sportster.

In the wake of the post-World War I recession, Cole began losing money. The success of the low-cost, mass-produced, cars had cut the volume of Cole-class cars by 50 percent. Cole, a conservative businessman, took steps to liquidate early in 1925 while the company was still solvent. The Cole Motor Car Company also made history by providing the first presidential automobile to President William Howard Taft in 1910.

Empire

In 1909, four of the biggest names in Indianapolis--Arthur C. Newby, president of the National Motor Vehicle Company; Carl C. Fisher, founder of Prest-O-Lite; James A. Allison, co-founder of Prest-O-Lite; and Robert Hassler from National--decided to build a sprightly two-passenger car for $800 known as The Little Aristocrat by The Empire Motor Car Company (1909-1911). Unfortunately, three of them--Newby, Fisher, and Allison, together with Frank H.

continued on page 34

Behind the wheel

Recreational activities, like auto touring, were largely responsible for the revival of U.S. 40, also known as The National Road, as a major transportation artery. Similar to other routes in the early 1900s, the roadbed that serviced wagons and coaches was no longer satisfactory, and motorists clamored for paved and wider roads. The National Old Trails Association was formed in 1913 to mark the auto trail and convince local and state officials to improve it. In addition, an effort to link the National Road, lying east of the Mississippi River, with the Santa Fe Trail in the west was underway to create another transcontinental route like the Lincoln Highway.

In 1926 the Old National Road became the new U.S. 40. By 1935 it was widened to serve the increased traffic, and facilities like motels, diners and gasoline stations sprung up across the route to serve the motorists. But the interstate system, particularly when Interstate 70 was built in the 1960s, changed the importance of U.S. 40. Motorists increasingly chose the speedy access offered by I-70, and U.S. 40 and its attending businesses suffered.

A reminder of the early days of U.S. 40 is on The Old Trails Building, formerly the headquarters of the Old Trails Auto Insurance Company and former home to the state auto license bureau. Near the intersection of Senate and Washington streets in Indianapolis, the building's facade is a collage of icons representing the route's past.

* * * * * *

In 1933, the Marmon Company in Indianapolis faced an ignoble end—bankruptcy. A major creditor was William Ansted, owner of Metal Auto Products which manufactured auto parts for Marmon.

The day that Ansted realized that Marmon received the final blow, he had all Marmon's overdue bills tallied, a total of $70,000. With the invoices in hand, Ansted went directly to the Marmon factory to negotiate some kind of settlement. Payment came in the form of some tools and the last Marmon car made, priced at $5,000.

Anstead enjoyed relating the story and boasting about having purchased the most expensive car, a nearly $70,000 price tag, to date.

Wheeler of Wheeler-Schebler Carburetor--also decided to build a two-and-a-half-mile oval on Indianapolis's west side to help improve the American automobile industry and had their attention diverted from the Empire auto firm. The first car to try out the track was the new Empire, the first one off the line. Late in 1911 The Empire Motor Car Company was sold to another group of Indianapolis businessmen, who renamed it Empire Automobile Company.

This company decided to contract for all parts and final assembly of its Empire Automobile by Rex Wheel Works of Connersville with assistance from Central Manufacturing, which received the contract for the bodies and the Rex Manufacturing Company, which made the tops and enclosures (both of Connersville). In July 1915, the company acquired the former Federal Motors plant in Indianapolis for production. By now, Little Aristocrats had outgrown their name with Teetor-Harley four-cylinder and Continental six-cylinder engines and prices ranging to $1,360. In 1919, The Greenville Car Company of Greenville, Pennsylvania bought the Empire name and designs.

Parry

The Parry was built by Parry Auto Company (1910-1911) as a two- or five-passenger, open car with 20 or 30 hp, four-cylinder ohv engines. After reorganization as Motor Car Manufacturing Company (1911-1912), the name was changed to New Parry. The last models, with four-cylinder engines developing 35 hp, were priced at $1,750.

The Pathfinder introduced in 1912 succeeded the New Parry and, as a boattail speedster, was noted for several advanced body innovations, such as the disappearing top, and spare-wheel cover. The various models were large with up to 132 in. wheelbases. Initially Pathfinders had four-cylinder engines, followed by sixes with V radiators. The company was reorganized as The Pathfinder Company (1915-1917). In 1916 a model with a Weidley 12-cylinder engine called Pathfinder the Great, King of Twelves, was launched. In December 1917 the company was liquidated in receivership.

Stutz

Five weeks before the Inaugural 500 mile race on Memorial Day 1911, Harry C. Stutz built his first race car. Capitalizing on the publicity generated by its eleventh place showing in the first outing at the 1911 race, Stutz formed the Ideal Motor Company to build a production version of the racer later that year. Its slogan was "The Car that Made Good in a Day." The sporty roadster made the company profitable. In 1912, the Ideal Motor Company and the Stutz Auto Parts Company merged to form the Stutz Motor Company. Harry C. Stutz's most famous passenger car was the Bearcat speedster of 1914. It followed the usual Stutz recipe of a low-slung chassis, a large engine (Wisconsin T-head, with four cylinders, producing 60 hp at 1,500 rpm), and other bare necessities, hood, fenders, raked steering column, two bucket seats, a fuel tank behind them, and wire-spoke wheels. A Stutz-made, three-speed transmission was integral with the differential, an uncommon feature at the time. This component had been designed and marketed by the Stutz Auto Parts Company before Stutz made complete cars.

The Stutz Bearcat was the most popular car in spite of its $2,000 price tag. Its appeal was boosted by Stutz's success at the race track. Bearcats finished fourth and sixth at the Indianapolis 500 in 1912 and won 25 of the 30 races in which they were entered that year. The next year a Bearcat finished second at the Indianapolis 500. In the years preceding World War I, Stutz's sales increased nearly ten fold--from 266 cars in 1912 to 2,207 five years later.

In 1915, Alan A. Ryan gained financial control of the company. Stutz became disenchanted with Ryan's regime, sold his interest in the company in 1919 and left to form H.C.S. Motor Company. (*See H.C.S. for the continuation of the Harry C. Stutz story.*)

In 1922 Charles M. Schwab, chairman of Bethlehem Steel, bought Ryan's stock. He viewed the Stutz company as a challenging new outlet for his patronage of artistic creativity, and he provided the money and guidance for the firm to rescue itself from the recession of the early 1920s. Under his supervision, the company began to design and build its own engines for the first time.

Late in 1924 Schwab installed Frederic E. Moskovics, formerly with Marmon and Franklin, as president. Moskovics' team quickly prepared a new design that discarded most links with the past and also formed the basis for all Stutz's future developments. The result was the 1926 Vertical Eight, or Safety Stutz. The base of the car was Charles R. "Pop" Greuter's 92-hp, straight-eight engine with chain-driven, single-overhead camshaft, and dual ignition, including two spark plugs per cylinder. The engine employed a one-piece casting of cylinders and crankcase in state-of-the-art fashion. The chassis featured four-wheel hydraulic brakes, an underslung worm-drive differential, and centralized chassis lubrication. This configuration allowed the fitting of lowbuilt, attractive bodies with safety glass. A year's free passenger insurance was included with each Safety Stutz.

The company introduced the Black Hawk speedsters in 1927. These low and short open types had reduced coachwork with scant cycle fenders and step plates replaced the running boards. Their fast looks proved no illusion when they won the American Automobile Association Stock Car Championship in 1927 and 1928. A Black Hawk placed second at Twenty-Four Hours of LeMans after leading the Bentley team cars much of the way.

In 1931, Stutz introduced Greuter's dual overhead-camshaft, four-valves per cylinder, 156 hp, straight-eight engine, designated the DV 32, to compete with the new multi-cylinder cars being brought out by Lincoln, Cadillac, Marmon and others. The single-camshaft eight was renamed the SV16. With the DV32 a new Bearcat was listed in speedster form, and on a shorter chassis, as the Super Bearcat.

Meanwhile the depression was taking its toll of the smaller manufacturers who lacked the financial resources to survive. After record sales of 5,000 cars in 1926, Stutz business declined to 110 autos in 1933 and six in 1934. The company continued to manufacture a light delivery van called the Pak-Age-Car until April 23, 1938, when a federal court ordered liquidation. Charles Schwab could not save Stutz nor himself from bankruptcy.

Nyberg

The Nyberg by the Nyberg Automobile Works (1913-1914) was made in as many as four different models, ranging up to the Model 646. This was a seven-passenger car that used a six-cylinder, 332 c.i. engine and cost $2,100.

Herff-Brooks

Herff-Brooks Corporation produced the Herff-Brooks (1915-1916) as a light car with a four- or six-cylinder L-head engines of 40 and 50 hp respectively. The Six-50 roadster with three-speed transmission cost $1,375.

continued on page 38

Behind the wheel

One of the last grand cars made by Duesenberg was owned by pharmaceutical baron Eli Lilly, who purchased the Duesenberg in 1934. This streamlined coupe became the highest-priced car sold by Duesenberg, and the completed car, with the coach work built by the A.H. Walker Co., is said to have sold for $25,000

During World War II, the car saw duty overseas and, at one point, was used as a tow truck. Reports indicate that the car languished for years in a Long Island garage in New York until *Tonight Show* host Jay Leno discovered it. After years of negotiation, Leno bought the car in 1995 and had it restored to its nearly original condition by Duesenberg expert Randy Ema.

"There may be a few undiscovered Duesenbergs left, but this is the last of the wild ones," Ema said.

* * * * * *

One of the Indianapolis Motor Speedway's nicknames is The Brickyard, appropriately named because the track was paved with bricks after the first race in 1909 resulted in several deaths. Approximately 3.2 million paving bricks were laid in the track and remained the main surface until the 1930s when all but the main straightaway was paved with asphalt. Five different companies have been identified as providing the bricks, including The Wabash Clay Company.

Although the Veedersburg company has disbanded, the kiln and some of the buildings remain in this southern Indiana town. *–information from the pamphlet "The Brickyard: The legendary bricks of Indy" by John E. Blazier and Tom Rollings*

* * * * * *

During its history, the Indianapolis 500 race has resulted in such automotive improvements as the rearview mirror, balloon tires and ethyl gasoline.

* * * * * *

Hoosier Scout

Hoosier Cyclecar Company built the Hoosier Scout in 1914 as a tandem cyclecar with a typical two-cylinder, air-cooled engine. The drive was by a friction transmission and belts to the rear wheels. The only distinguishing feature of the body was its boattail.

Lyons-Knight

The Lyons-Knight automobile was a side business of the Atlas Engine Company, which manufactured large stationary diesel engines. The Lyons-Knight used both four- and six-cylinder engines. These large five and seven passenger autos had up to 130 inch wheelbases. Closed limousines were available at $4,300.

Hassler

The Hassler by Hassler Motor Co (1917) was a small car of short life and limited production, the Hassler was available only as a two-passenger roadster at a price of $1,650. It was powered by a four-cylinder Buda engine. Houk wire wheels were standard equipment. Front suspension was by two semielliptic springs clipped at midpoint. Rear suspension was by two semielliptic transverse springs with radius rods extending from the axle housing to the transmission.

H.C.S.

Harry C. Stutz sold his interest in the Stutz Motor Company in 1919 and left to form H.C.S. Motor Company. The H.C.S. was an expensive assembled automobile similar to its predecessor, the Stutz. Weidley four-cylinder and Midwest six-cylinder engines, produced in Indianapolis, were used. Stutz's timing was unfortunate. The economic recession of 1921-1922 had an unfortunate effect on the automobile industry. With declining auto sales, Stutz decided that the company should concentrate on taxi cab production in 1924. H.C.S. survived until 1927.

Duesenberg

During Duesenberg's tenure in Indianapolis, the company was incorporated under four names: Duesenberg Motor Distributing (1920-1925), Duesenberg Motors Company (1925-1926), Duesenberg Inc. (1926-1929) and Cord Corporation (1929-1937). The complex consisted of a 17-acre site at the southwest corner of Harding and West Washington streets. Previous to moving to here the Duesenberg brothers--Fred and August--built extremely high-quality and advanced engines and automobiles, but were seldom financially successful. Part of their reason for moving to Indianapolis was to return to their racing roots and be near the Indianapolis Motor Speedway where they had already enjoyed some success. The Speedway also could be used for testing their passenger cars as well as the racers.

Their most famous racer appeared in 1920, a 183 c.i., Bugatti-inspired, eight-cylinder engine with single-overhead camshaft and three valves per cylinder. It won the 1921 French Grand Prix. In the 1920s the racing cars were rivals of the Millers at Indianapolis Motor Speedway, and victory was assured in 1924 by the adoption of a centrifugal supercharger. Duesenberg enjoyed victories in 1925 and 1927. It is interesting that the Duesenberg racing operations were not officially supported by the auto production firm. The racing operations were located on the second floor of the Thompson Pattern Shop at 1532 West Washington Street, directly across the street from the factory (building still exists). This was a separate entity headed by August Duesenberg.

The first Duesenberg production car debuted at the end of 1920. This Model A was an extremely expensive, very advanced and luxurious car, which pioneered the use of straight eight-cylinder engines and four-wheel hydraulic brakes. The Model A was produced until 1926. In 1926, Errett Lobban Cord of Auburn acquired control of the company. He commissioned Fred Duesenberg to develop the ultimate motorcar that would outclass all American makes.

The Model J, introduced at the New York Automobile Salon for the 1929 model year, was the most remarkable automobile in America: bigger, faster, more elaborate and more expensive than any other. Its 420 c.i., eight-cylinder engine, made by Lycoming (a Cord Corporation firm), had dual overhead camshafts operating four valves per cylinder; a layout of racing type said to develop 265 bhp at 4,250 rpm. Although the complete car weighed more than 4,980 pounds, it was claimed to be capable of 116 mph in top gear and 89 mph in second.

In 1929, the cost of the long, low-built chassis was $8,500. Duesenbergs were very popular with all leading coach builders and the company preferred to sell cars complete with bodies designed by them but made by approved builders (i.e. Murphy, Bohman and

Schwartz, Judkins, Derham and LeBaron). In this form, catalogued models cost up to $18,000.

In 1932 a supercharged version of the Model J, the SJ, was added. A maximum speed of 129 mph was obtainable, with an acceleration figure of 0 to100 mph in 17 seconds.

Celebrity buyers included New York Mayor Jimrny Walker, William Randolph Hearst, Elizabeth Arden, Mae West, Gary Cooper and Clark Gable and the kings of Spain and Italy. The make survived the Depression but died in the collapse of the Cord Corporation in 1937. The total Model J production was 480, just 20 cars short of the projected 500.

Lafayette

The Lafayette Motors Company was formed in October 1919 with Charles W. Nash of Nash Motors as president. A large cadre of former Cadillac executives were involved with this venture. The Lafayette was a luxurious, lavishly equipped V8 designed by D. McCall White, who also did the 1915 Cadillac V8. Its L-head engine developed 90 hp at 2,750 rpm. It was produced in a variety of open and closed body styles beginning at $5,000. Its thermostatically controlled radiator shutters were a pioneering feature. Production began in August 1920 with the introduction of the "1921 Lafayette." As has been noted repeatedly in this book, the early 1920's were not the best of times to introduce any automobile, especially a luxury auto. Lafayette only sold 700 cars in the first year. In July 1922, Lafayette Motors was moved to Milwaukee, Wisconsin, to geographically consolidate Nash's operations.

Brooke-Spacke

The Brooke-Spacke cyclecar (1920-1921) by Spacke Machine & Tool Company had a two-cylinder air-cooled engine, which was used by many other cyclecar makers, but it catered to American taste with electric lighting and starting, plus three forward speeds. Later cars reverted to cyclecar tradition by using two-speed planetary transmission.

Frontenac

The Frontenac (1921-1925) was designed by Louis Chevrolet and Cornelius W. Van Ranst, who later contributed to the design of the Cord L-29. (The Chevrolet brothers, Arthur and Louis, owned a company in the late teens that made cylinder heads for Fords and racing cars called Fronty Fords.)

The Frontenac featured four-cylinder, single-overhead camshaft engine, with front and rear bumpers constructed as an integral part of the frame. The Frontenac Motor Company was capitalized for $1 million and secured the former Empire Motor Car Company plant for production. The Frontenac made its official debut at the 1922 Indianapolis 500. Unfortunately, the economic conditions at the time resulted in the inaugural Frontenac never reaching production. A second Frontenac of Chevrolet's design featured a 140 inch chassis with an 80 hp eight-cylinder engine. Again, because of financial problems, production never began.

Current auto makers

Today listed in the top 20 employers in Indianapolis are General Motors Corporation, Ford Motor Company and their direct descendants, including Allison Transmission Division GMC (heavy duty transmissions), Ford Motor Company (auto steering components) and General Motors Truck and Bus Group (metal stampings for trucks). Other automotive manufacturers are Navistar International (diesel engines), Arvin Industries (metal parts), Chrysler Corporation (engine foundry) and Alpine Electronics (automotive audio equipment).

Other Indianapolis facts:

• The Wheeler-Schebler Carburetor Company was founded by Frank Wheeler (one of the four founders of the Indianapolis Motor Speedway) and George Schebler. Schebler developed one of the first successful gasoline carburetors.
• The town of Speedway was founded by Carl G. Fisher in 1912 as a "horseless city" to provide housing for workers at his Prest-O-Lite plant and future manufacturers' plants.
• Fred Duesenberg helped perfect freewheeling, the over-running clutch and the syncromesh transmission.
• With his proceeds from the sale of Prest-O-Lite, James A. Allison started Allison Engineering Company, predecessor of today's Allison Engine Company Division of Rolls-Royce and Allison Transmission Division of GMC.
• Ford Motor Company assembled autos in its plant at 1307 East Washington Street from 1914-1932.

Roadside attractions

The Youth Education and Historical Center, sponsored by the Indiana State Police, has a collection of ISP cars.
8500 E. 21st Street, 317-899-8293
Hours: Monday through Friday, 8-11 a.m. and 1-4 p.m.

The Indianapolis Raceway Park is a multipurpose facility featuring drag, oval and road racing. The site is home to the U.S. Nationals Drag Race.
10267 E. State Route 136, 800-884-6472, call for schedule

The Indianapolis Motor Speedway was built in 1909 as a proving ground and racetrack for automobiles. Today the track hosts the Indianapolis 500 race and NASCAR's Brickyard 400. A tour by bus around the 2.5-mile oval is also available when the track is not in use, weather permitting.
4790 W. 16th Street, 317-484-6747
Hours: daily, 9 a.m. to 5 p.m., closed December 25

The IMS Hall of Fame Museum displays many of the races' winning cars, memorabilia, antique automobiles and equipment. A film on the track's history is also shown in the Tony Hulman Theatre.
4790 W. 16th Street, 317-484-6747
Hours: daily, 9 a.m. to 5 p.m., closed Dec. 25

The Indiana State Museum has an eclectic collection of Indianapolis 500 and automotive memorabilia, which is part of a rotating display. Highlights include 500 race participants' uniforms, Mike Mosley's 1981 Indy car and a 1927 Stutz Model AA.
202 N. Alabama Street, (a new facility is being built) 317-232-1637
Hours: Monday through Saturday, 9 a.m. to 4:45 p.m.;
Sunday, noon to 4:45 p.m.
closed Jan. 1, Easter, Thanksgiving and December 25

The Library of the Indiana Historical Society contains rare books, manuscripts, maps and pictures relating to the state's history. Information available on request.
315 W. Ohio Street (currently in Indiana State Library), 317-940-9333
Hours: Monday through Friday, 8 a.m. to 4:30 p.m.; Saturday, 8 a.m. to 4 p.m. (closed on Saturday during the summer)
closed on holidays

Many of the buildings that housed the movers and shakers of the automotive industry still stand--some in disrepair and others showing well-maintained and/or refurbished exteriors. The following lists the former companies and addresses of their facilities. Most are privately owned.

Name	Address
Alena Steam Products	230 E. 16th Street
Allison Engineering Co.	1230-40 Main Street
James A. Allison Mansion	3200 Cold Spring Road
American Motor Car Co.	1959 S. Meridian Street
Atlas Engine Works/	1901 Rev. Andrew J.
Midwest Engine Co.	Brown Avenue
Buick Showroom	1302 N. Meridian Street
Cadillac Co. of Indiana Showroom	500-514 N. Capitol Ave.
Carr Building-Showroom	5442 E. Washington Street
Carson Motor Co. Showroom	1127-29 Shelby Street
Charles E. Stutz Automobile Sales Co.	850 N. Meridian Street
Cole Motor Car Co.	730 E. Washington Street
Diamond Chain Co.	402 Kentucky Avenue
Duesenberg Motor Car Co.	1511 W. Washington St.
Frederick S. Duesenberg Home	3316 Fall Creek Parkway
Carl G. Fisher Mansion (Fisher Hall)	3060 Cold Spring Road
Ford Motor Co.	1307-23 E. Washington St.
Gates/Masters Co.	431 N. Capitol Avenue
Gibson Co. Building (Fisher affiliation)	433-447 N. Capitol Ave.
Goodyear Tire and Rubber Co.	640 N. Capitol Avenue
HCS Motor Car Co.	1402 N. Capitol Avenue
Harry Hyatt, Graham-Paige Showroom	1327 N. Capitol Avenue
Hassler Motor Co.	1535 E. Naomi Street
Frank Hatfield Ford Co. Showroom	627 N. Capitol Avenue
Ideal Motor Car Co.	212 W. 10th Street
Indianapolis Motor Speedway	4790 W. 16th Street
Lafayette Motor Co.	2745 S. Holt Road

Lauth Chevrolet Co. Showroom	3547 E. Washington Street
Lexington Automobile Co. Showroom	1200 N. Meridian Street
Link-Belt Co./Ewart Plant	220 S. Belmont Street
Marion/Empire Motor Car Co.	323 W. 15th Street
Maxwell-Briscoe Motor Co. Showroom	363-365 N. Illinois Street
National Motor Vehicle Co.	1101-47 E. 22nd Street
Nordyke & Marmon Co. Plant 3	1 blk w. of Kentucky Ave. & Morris St.
Premier Motor Manufacturing Co.	3500 E. 20th Street
Stutz Motor Car Co.	1008 N. Capitol Avenue
Sullivan Motor Sales Co. Showroom	646-680 Virginia Avenue
Thompson Pattern Shop -Duesenberg Racing Operations	1532 W. Washington St.
William N. Thompson Mansion (president of Stutz, house is also former Governor's mansion)	4343 N. Meridian Street
Wheeler-Schebler Carburetor Co.	1234-36 Barth Avenue
Frank Wheeler/Stokely Mansion	3040 Cold Spring Road
William Small Co., Monroe factory	602 N. Capitol Avenue
Williams Building Showroom	611-17 N. Capitol Avenue
Grover Winnings Chrysler Showroom	1625 E. Washington St.

Source: David L. Baker, Indianapolis-Marion County Automobile Industry, Indianapolis, Indianapolis Historic Preservation Commission, c 1990. All sites exist per author's verification, June 1997.

Jasper

Jasper Engines & Transmissions was founded in 1942, and today is the nation's largest mass remanufacturer of a diverse line of drive-train components. Annual production includes 50,000 gas engines, 15,000 transmissions, 5,000 diesel engines, 1,500 differentials and rear axle assemblies, and 1,500 stern drives. The company's product mix also includes performance engines and transmissions, marine engines, alternate fuel engines and conversion systems and electric motors.

Kokomo

Today Kokomo's primary industry is related to the automobile, although no cars are manufactured here. But the town's early history of automotive manufacturing is marked with distinction.

Commercial automobile production in Kokomo, and concurrently in the United States, began with the first recorded sale of a Haynes-Apperson automobile in the fall of 1896 (Out-of-staters Duryea and Winton also record sales in 1896.) Elwood Haynes' historic demonstration of his Pioneer automobile along Pumpkinvine Pike on July 4, 1894, preceded commercial production by two years. In a span of 30 years, four different motor vehicles were built in Kokomo ending with both the Haynes and the Apperson in 1925.

Kokomo's automotive history began with the Sintz engine that Haynes discovered at the Chicago World's Fair in the summer of 1893. Haynes ordered a one-horsepower engine in the fall of 1893. The engine was mounted on sawhorses in the Haynes' kitchen, and the gasoline and battery connections were installed. After much cranking the engine started. The machine "ran with such speed and vibration that it pulled itself from its attachments to the floor. Luckily, however, one of the battery wires was wound around the motor shaft and this disconnected the current," according to Haynes' *The Complete Motorist*. Shortly afterwards, Haynes made arrangements with Elmer Apperson to work in the privacy of Apperson's Riverside Machine Works. Moreover, the intense vibration of the engine prompted Haynes to design and build a much heavier carriage frame than he had planned originally.

According to author Ralph Gray, "Haynes had conceived the idea, drawn up the plans, purchased the engine, worked out the engineering problems--using the higher mathematics he had acquired so laboriously at Worcester Polytechnic Institute in Massachusetts, and financed the entire project. The Apperson brothers and their workmen built the car. The Appersons made modifications and offered various suggestions as the work progressed. But primary credit is usually attributed to Haynes."

While there remains some question about who actually built the first car in America, only the Haynes was advertised as "America's First Car." This claim was based on the grounds that the 1893 Duryea was only a motorized buggy.

In 1895, Haynes and the Apperson brothers formed an informal partnership and set about building a new car especially for the *Times-Herald* race in Chicago, the first automobile race in America. The new Haynes-Apperson auto was unable to start the *Times-Herald* race because it was damaged in an accident while proceeding to the starting line on race day morning. The Haynes-Apperson entry received a $150 prize for its meritorious design feature--the reduction of vibration by balancing the engine.

The Haynes-Apperson Company was incorporated in 1898 and set out to dramatically increase its production. Elmer Apperson resigned from the Haynes-Apperson Company on November 15, 1901. The firm was not reorganized until 1905, and the corporate name was then changed to the Haynes Automobile Company. Haynes relinquished direct managerial control to V.E. Minich to allow the inventor to devote more time to metallurgical research.

In 1903, *Horseless Age* reported on a few changes on the Haynes. Not only had a steering wheel replaced the lever, but it was designed so that the entire steering column could be tilted forward out of the way of driver or passenger upon entering or leaving the vehicle. Today we might refer to this feature as the tilt steering wheel.

Near the end of 1908, the Kokomo *Morning Dispatch* reported that 600 employees were capable of producing 400 cars a year (actual production for 1908 and 1909 amounted to approximately 350 cars each year). The "oldest automobile factory in the United States" manufactured two grades of automobiles--the five-passenger, 30-hp

continued on page 48

Behind the wheel

American pioneers of the internal-combustion automobile include J. Frank and Charles E. Duryea (1893), Elwood Haynes (1894), Alexander Winton (1896), Ransom E. Olds (1896), Charles B. King (1896) and Henry Ford (1896). J. Frank Duryea, by his own account, produced his first operable machine in September 1893, in Springfield, Massachusetts. Evidence for Duryea's claim is substantiated by a story in the town's newspaper, *Republican*, on September 22, 1893. The article describes the initial, rather disappointing test run.

By any reckoning, however, the second successful automobile in America, and to Haynes's way of thinking the first complete and satisfactory model, was the one he test drove on July 4, 1894.

* * * * * * * *

Elwood Haynes is often credited with inventing the first successful spark-ignition automobile. The initial road test was on July 4,1894 on Pumpkinvine Pike in Kokomo.

Yet, perhaps the best way to phrase his contribution to automotive history is provided by a 1994 article in *Traces*, a publication of the Indiana Historical Society: "Elwood Haynes was widely recognized as the proprietor and inventive genius behind the oldest automobile company in America, something that Haynes Automobile Company advertising people interpreted to mean also the first such company in America."

His creative inventiveness also extended into metallurgy. He is rightfully credited with developing one of the first types of stainless steel. His motivation for this discovery stemmed from his wife's request for silverware that wouldn't tarnish.

Another of his inventions is still used today—Stellite. Harder than steel and resistant of corrosion, Stellite is used in space exploration and for other highly corrosive environments.

* * * * * *

runabout selling for $2,500 and the seven-passenger, 50 hp touring car priced at $5,500. In 1911, Haynes became the first company to equip an open car with a top, a windshield, head lamps and a speedometer as standard equipment. The 1914 Haynes was one of the first to offer the Vulcan Electric Gear Shift as standard equipment.

By September 1920, the company completed a new four-story assembly building, 500 feet by 150 feet, complete with a moving assembly line in the 1100 block of South Home Avenue. (The building stands today.) At one point the assembly line reached a maximum production rate of 60 cars a day. The company also began to build its own automobile bodies in 1920 and in 1921 boasted that its cars were at least "90 percent Kokomo-made." This post-war exuberance was followed by the contraction of the market for the type of autos that Haynes produced. Manufacturing at the Haynes plants ceased on September 2, 1924.

The Apperson Brothers Automobile Company produced its first car in 1902, building perhaps a dozen for the year. It is said that Elmer Apperson's passion for speed and open spaces inspired the Jack Rabbit insignia first seen on 1906 racers. The Appersons continued their interest in auto racing, and their autos competed in a number of events including two Indianapolis 500 races. Apperson Plant One was built on the site of the original Apperson Riverside Machine Works in 1910. Plant Two was constructed in the 1700 block of North Washington Street (now a Delco Electronics plant). The corporate offices were completed across the street from this plant.

The company enjoyed its peak year in 1919, employing about 600 people and producing 3,000 units at the two plants. In the early 1920's, business began to decrease. The Appersons, like many others, were not competitive with the larger manufacturers. Production ceased in 1925, thus ending the pioneering saga of Haynes and Appersons.

The Haynes and Apperson plants provided a transition for Kokomo as an integral part of the American automotive industry. Crosley Radio renovated the Haynes Auto body plant at the northeast corner of Firmin and Home avenues in 1936. Delco Radio Division of General Motors purchased this facility eight months later.

In 1938, Delco Radio introduced the first push-button car radio. For more than half a century, Delco Electronics (name changed in

Kokomo dubs itself as the City of Firsts, and the following automotive accomplishments are included in the claims.

1894　First commercially-built automobile built by Elwood Haynes.

1894　First pneumatic rubber tire invented by D.C. Spraker, then president of Kokomo Rubber Tire Co.

1902　First carburetor for a gas-powered vehicle developed by George Kingston.

1938　First push-button car radio developed at Delco Radio Division of General Motors Corp.

1947　First signal-seeking car radio developed at Delco Radio Division of General Motors Corp.

1957　First all-transistor car radio developed at Delco Radio Division of General Motors Corp.

1970) has supplied electronic components for the automotive industry. Today Delco is Kokomo's largest employer.

The Chrysler Corporation opened its first Kokomo facility at the old Haynes Auto plant at 1100 Home Avenue in 1937 to produce manual transmissions. The company built a new transmission plant on U.S. 31 and concurrently closed its Home Avenue facilities in 1965. Later Chyrsler also erected a new casting plant at 1001 Boulevard. Chrysler continues to expand its Kokomo facilities. All transmissions for Chrysler automobiles are made in Kokomo.

In 1998 Chyrsler will open the electronic transmission plant located north on U.S. 31. At full production, all three Chyrsler plants will employ about 8,500 workers.

Roadside attractions

In nearby Burlington, Dave's Hubcaps offers nearly 42,000 hubcaps from the 1920s to the present for sale.
west of Kokomo on State Route 22
765-566-3062

The Elwood Haynes Museum houses three Haynes automobiles dating from 1905 to 1924 as well as reams of material on the inventor often credited with the first ignition-sparked automobile.
1915 S. Webster Street
765-456-7500
Hours: Tuesday through Saturday, 1 to 4 p.m.
Sunday, 1 to 5 p.m.
closed on holidays

Seiberling Mansion/The Howard County Historical Museum offers both a look at late-Victorian architecture and antique cars. A.G. Seiberling played an instrumental role in developing the Haynes and Apperson automobiles.
1200 W. Sycamore Street, 765-452-4314
Hours: closed January
Tuesday through Sunday, 1-4 p.m.

The City of Firsts Automotive Heritage Museum is one of the state's newest attractions, opening in late 1997. The 40,000 square-foot museum will feature Kokomo-built cars as well as other objects celebrating automotive heritage.
northeast corner of U.S. 31 and North Street, 765-454-9999
Hours: TBA

A historical marker commemorating the first Haynes run is at the northeast corner of East Boulevard and Goyer Street.

The former homes of Elmer Apperson and Edgar Apperson still stand at 408 W. Mulberry Street and 518 West Walnut Street, respectively. Both houses are privately owned.

Did you know?
The National Automotive and Truck Museum of the United States in Auburn displays the truck that holds the world's land-speed record for trucks. Called the Endeavor, the truck is built on a modified International Harvester chassis and has set speed records on the Bonneville salt flats in Utah.

Lafayette

The American Motor Vehicle Company built two models: the American, also known as the American Junior, (1916-1920) and the Dumore (1918). The American was an ultra-light cyclecar with a single-cylinder engine. The Dumore was a two-passenger cyclecar with a four-cylinder engine.

In 1989, Subaru Isuzu Automotive, Inc. became the first foreign automobile venture to build a plant in Indiana, choosing Lafayette for its location. This modern plant produces the Subaru Legacy (1989 to present), Isuzu trucks and the Trooper sport utility vehicles (1989 to present) and the Honda Passport (1994 to present). This facility produces 240,000 vehicles annually.

Lafayette's automotive-component companies include Fairfield Manufacturing (gears, shafts, and differentials) and Ross Gear Division of TRW Inc. (manual and power steering gears). (Sidenote: Purdue University's Ross-Ade stadium in West Lafayette attributes half its name to Davis Ross, the inventor of an improved steering gear for automobiles.)

Roadside attractions

The Imagination Station encourages innovate thinking through interactive exhibits. A 1910 Maxwell automobile is one of the tools that the center uses to encourage scientific exploration for children of all ages.
600 N. 4th Street, 765-420-7780
Hours: Friday through Sunday, 1-5 p.m.

The Red Crown Mini-Museum is a converted Standard Oil station featuring auto memorabilia, particularly those items related to vintage gas stations.
corner of 6th and South streets, 765-742-0280
call for appointment

In nearby Frankfort, The Goodwin Funeral Home houses a private collection that includes the race car that won the 1931 Indianapolis 500, a 1947 Tucker and other significant automobiles.
200 S. Main Street, 765-654-5533
call for appointment

LaPorte

The Munson Electric Motor Company produced the Munson from 1899 to 1902. The Munson may have been the first gasoline-electric hybrid made in America. Two- and four-cylinder engines were used for this chassis and running gear product. The Munson chassis was fitted with the body of the buyer's choice.

Roadside attractions

Door Prairie Museum contains automotive treasures spanning 100 years. Featured automobiles are a1886 Benz Motor Wagon, a 1912 Baker Electric, a 1914 Mitchell, a 1929 Duesenberg, a 1937 Cord, a 1948 Tucker and a 1982 DeLorean.
2405 Indiana Avenue, 219-326-1337
Hours: April to December, closed major holidays
Tuesday through Saturday, 10 a.m. to 4:30 p.m.; Sunday, noon to 4:30 p.m.

In nearby Michigan City, The Great Lakes Museum of Military History displays an assortment of military memorabilia including vehicles.
1710 E. U.S. 20, 219-872-2702
Hours: May through Labor Day
Tuesday through Friday, 9 a.m. to 4 p.m.; Saturday, 10 a.m. to 4 p.m.; Sunday, noon to 4 p.m.
Labor Day through May--closed on Sunday

Lawrenceburg

In 1909, the J. & M. Motor Car Company produced the James Model A roadster. It was a highwheeler with 38-inch rear wheels and 36-inch front wheels, powered by an air-cooled, two-cylinder engine, and sold in the $700 to $800 price range. In 1911, J. & M. made a four-cylinder model called the Dearborn. The company shortly discontinued making automobiles.

Did you know?

The petroleum industry was a principle sponsor in building the Lincoln Heritage Trail in southern Indiana to encourage driving.

Ligonier

Located along the Lincoln Highway in northwestern Noble county, the small town of Ligonier was the home of two automobile models manufactured by the Mier Carriage & Buggy Company from 1903 to 1910. They were the Star (1903-1904) and the Mier (1908-1910).

Solomon Mier was one of the early Jewish immigrants from Germany who arrived in Ligonier in 1854. Through the years, he owned a number of businesses including a general store, a bank, and a carriage and buggy company which built fancy carriages. The building still exists on the northwest corner of Lincoln Way west and Cavin Street (which turns into Lincoln Way south).

The Mier Automobile catalog of 1908 lists Model A and B Runabouts retailing for $575 f.o.b. Ligonier, Indiana. Advertising copy described the Runabout as "a motor vehicle containing all the features of a high-priced automobile less their disadvantages, and in short is a runabout that is especially adapted for the business and professional man." The Runabouts were very competitively priced vehicles. Unfortunately a competitive price is only one of the factors in achieving a commercial success.

Roadside attractions

The Solomon Mier Manor has been converted into a bed and breakfast inn. The house is considered a good example of Victorian architecture. Guided tours are available by appointment.
508 South Cavin Street, 219-984-3668
call for reservations and rates

Visitors familar with The Auburn Cord Duesenberg Museum will recognize one of its former displays. The museum's collection of antique and classic radios has been relocated to the Indiana Historical Radio Museum at 800 Lincoln Way south (three blocks south of the Solomon Mier Manor). The museum is home to over 400 antique and classic radios, from the early crystal sets to the first transistor radio.

Logansport

The Bendix Company built the Bendix from 1908 to 1909. The Bendix 30 was a highwheeler with a four-cylinder, water-cooled engine, solid tires, and sold for $1,500.

Perhaps the best known Logansport automobile is the ReVere, built by the ReVere Motor Car Corporation (1918-1926). Auto racers Gil Anderson, Tom Mooney (noted team drivers for Stutz and Premier respectively) and Adolph Monsen collaborated on the design of the high-powered, high-performance ReVere. The car utilized the Duesenberg four-cylinder, 90-hp, "walking-beam" engine, which was so named because of the horizontal valve arrangement that used extremely long vertical rocker arms (walking-beams). ReVere's 1920 Foursome was the epitome of sportiness with bullet head lamps, slanted windshield, step plates, cycle fenders, wire wheels, and side-mounted tires. A white custom-built Foursome with Victoria top was ordered by King Alfonso XIII of Spain. ReVere's slogan was "America's Incomparable Car." Innovations for 1925 included an optional Continental six-cylinder engine. The last model in 1926 may have anticipated power steering with dual steering wheels, one for normal driving and one for parking. The ReVere organization saw six changes of management in eight years and faded after 1926.

Today Logansport's chief automotive enterprises are Diversitech General (automotive vibration isolators), Exide Corporation (auto batteries), Modine (radiators), T.M. Morris (wiring assemblies), Rockwell International (springs), and Switches, Inc. (starter solenoids and ignition coils.)

Marion

The Marion Crosley plant is known for its post World War II production of the Crosley (1946-1952). Corporate headquarters of Crosley Motors Inc. was in Cincinnati, Ohio. At its peak, Crosley produced a wide range of vehicles including sedans, station wagons, delivery vans and several sports models. The Hotshot model won races at Sebring and elsewhere. Crosley showed the influence of European economy and sports cars, though it was a bit too austere for American tastes. The plant at 1700 Factory Avenue is now occupied by Diversitech General and produces reinforced plastic components automotive components.

Marion's other automotive connections include Dana Corporation's Spicer Universal Joint Division, which produces universal joints and drive shafts, and General Motors' CPC Group, which makes auto body and sheet metal stampings.

McCordsville

The Columbia Electric Company manufactured a car known as the Leader from 1905-1906. In Knightstown, Leader Manufacturing Company then produced the car from 1906-1912. Early Leader models had two-cylinder enginers and sliding-gear transmissions.

Mishawaka

The Simplex Motor Car Company manufactured the American Simplex (1906-1910) and the Amplex (1910-1913). Originally the American Simplex used a four-cylinder, two-stroke, 40-hp engine. Later increased to 415 c.i. and rated at 50 hp, the two-stroke engine was advertised as having "no valves because it doesn't need them." For 1910, three open models and two closed versions were offered, with prices up to $5,400. The model name was changed to Amplex to avoid confusion with another Simplex built by a New York firm. In 1913, the company called it quits after two reorganizations.

In 1984, auto production returned to Indiana with the introduction of the Hummer by AM General Corporation. The company traces two lines of genealogy: 1. to Overland Auto of Terre Haute and then Indianapolis, by way of Willys-Overland of Toledo, Ohio, predecessor of Kaiser-Jeep, and 2. to the Studebaker Corporation of South Bend and its military truck division, purchased by Kaiser-Jeep in 1964. Kaiser-Jeep became AM General in 1970.

The Hummer, more than 15 feet long and seven feet wide, is manufactured at 13200 McKinley Highway. Total production exceeds 110,000 delivered to the Army, Marines, and more than 20 nations abroad. For civilian use the Hummer is modified with a more powerful 396 c.i. diesel engine, bucket seats, impact-restraint doors,

continued on page 57

Behind the wheel

At the begin of the century, highway signs were almost nonexistent. In order to help participants in road tours, local American Automobile Associations would send out a pilot car to mark the route with confetti. However, pandemonium erupted during one road rally when the pilot car ran out of confetti midway between South Bend and Chicago.

For a substitute, the driver bought a supply of corn and beans from a nearby farm. His corn-and-bean trail, however, drew hundreds of chickens into the path of surprised motorists.

"I followed the clearest trail that I have found since leaving home," said the tour's chairman, "and it wasn't corn and beans either. It was chicken feathers."

* * * * * *

In 1911, the Indianapolis Motor Speedway was built for a theoretical speed of 61 miles per hour. The theoretical speed limit is the point where the car begins to skid. That, however, is not the practical and actual limit of speed that can be attained on the 2.5-mile track. Top speed officially recorded during the oval's history is 237.498 mph set by Arie Luyendyk on May 11, 1996.

* * * * *

The first Mishawaka-made HUMMERs were built in 1984 for the U.S. Army to replace the Jeep. But with the decline of military spending and the end of the Cold War, the manufacturer, AM General, realized it had to develop civilian and export markets. Movie star Arnold Schwarzenegger was the first civilian to buy a HUMMER. Today, the vehicles are being sold on car lots throughout the country.

* * * * * *

halogen headlights and AM/FM stereo. Air conditioning is a dealer option. The Hummer is billed as "The Most Serious 4 x 4 on Earth."

Muncie

Automobile manufacturing in Muncie started with its namesake--the Muncie--in 1903 and closed out with the Durant in 1928. In this span of 25 years, five different motor vehicles such as the Interstate, Rider-Lewis, Sheridan and Star were built.

Large-scale automobile manufacturing started in 1908 thanks to the efforts of the Commercial Club of Muncie (forerunner to the Chamber of Commerce). A group spearheaded by the five Ball brothers--George A., Frank C., William C., Edmund F., and Dr. Lucius L.--along with J.M. Marling and Tom Hart formed the Interstate Motor Company. A two-building plant three blocks long went up on the site at the end of West Willard Street.

The first Interstate models used a 287 c.i., four-cylinder engine. In 1912, features included electric lighting, starting, and fuel pump. These models were on three different chassis. Interstate was reorganized as the Interstate Motor Company in 1914, and the four-cylinder Model 45 was offered. The Interstate T was offered from 1915 to 1918. The Interstate put Muncie on the auto-maker's map staying in production until 1918.

The Interstate plant was acquired by General Motors in 1919. The Sheridan was produced at this site by the Sheridan Motor Car Company, a unit of GM, during 1920 and 1921. The Sheridan used a four-cylinder Northway engine and sold for less than $2,000. It was slotted to fill the gap between the Chevrolet and the Oakland cars in the GM line-up. William C. Durant took over the facility in 1921 to form Durant Motors, Inc.

Three makes of autos were produced in this plant from 1922 to 1928: Durant (1922-28), Princeton (1923-24) and Star (1923). The Durant Six used an Ansted engine from Connersville. The Princeton also used the Ansted engine and was Durant's attempt to produce a car between his Flint and Locomobile lines. The Star was inexpensive and lightweight like the Ford Model T. The Star touring car had a 134 c.i. four-cylinder Continental engine and was priced at $443.

Auto manufacturing in Muncie ended in 1928.

In 1928, the Durant facility made the transition to producing automotive supplies when the Delco-Remy Division of General Motors acquired it to make Delco batteries. By 1934, the Muncie plant was supplying all GM cars and trucks. The plant produced its 100 millionth battery in 1965. A new battery plant at 4500 S. Delaware Road replaced this facility in 1976. The plant is now known as Delphi Energy & Engine Management Systems–Muncie.

General Motors also bought the original Warner Gear plant at 1200 W. 8th Street in 1919 and established the Muncie Products Division to supply transmissions for Oakland, Pontiac, Oldsmobile, and GMC Truck. This plant was credited with large-volume production of synchromesh transmissions that were adopted throughout GM's auto lines between 1928 and 1932. The Depression forced closing of the plant in 1932. Three years later it re-opened as Chevrolet-Muncie, and the plant has been enlarged several times since. When GM celebrated its 75th anniversary in September 1983, the plant occupied 1.2 million square feet on 62.5 acres. In 1990, the GM operation at this facility, known as Muncie Hydra-Matic, merged with Chrysler Acustar operations to form New Venture Gear Inc.

Tom W. and Harry Warner, Abbott L. and J.C. Johnson, Col. William Hitchcock and Thomas Morgan founded Warner Gear Company of Muncie in 1900. Warner Gear's first major contribution to the industry was the differential. The company also produced transmissions, steering gears and rear axles and had broad appeal among the nation's automobile makers. Warner was the first company to develop a standardized three-speed transmission in 1926. It could be mass produced at half the cost of specialty transmissions and was suitable for use in almost any automobile. This successful innovation saved the company during a time when specialty manufacturers across the country were closing their doors. A merger with Borg & Beck, Marvel Carburetor, Mechanics Universal Joint Company, Wheeler-Schebler (Indianapolis), and several others in 1928 created Borg Warner Corporation. Warner Gear has altered its product line several times to stay abreast of market opportunities. Production originated in the former Warner Arc Light Co. plant at 1200 W. 8th Street. The company purchased a whole city block on Seymour Avenue for a major expansion in 1918. In 1930 the division built the first part of what is today its headquarters at 5401 Kilgore

Avenue. Several additions and changes preceded the consolidation of Warner Gear activities at this location and the concurrent closing of its Seymour Avenue facilities in 1977.

Roadside attractions near Muncie

In Albany, the Muncie Dragway is the site of national drag strip competitions, including The Winston World Title Drag Series.
765-789-6831, call for schedule

In Bryant, the Bearcreek Farms' Tin Lizzie Museum has more than 10 early-model Ford cars. Alongside each car is information about its history.
8330 North 400 East, 219-997-6822
Hours: Tuesday through Sunday, 8 a.m. to 5 p.m.

In Portland, a marker indicating the site of Elwood Haynes birthplace is located on the grounds of the Williamson Spencer Funeral Home.
208 N. Commerce

New Albany

The American Automobile Manufacturing Company built the American with a two-stroke engine in 1911 and 1912. It appears that American was later connected with the Ohio Falls Motor Company that made the Ohio Falls (1913-1914) and the Pilgrim (1913-1914).

The Hercules Motor Car Company produced the Crown (1914) and the Hercules (1914). The Crown was a two-passenger cyclecar with a 104 c.i., four-cylinder engine and friction transmission, priced at $385. The Hercules was a four-passenger auto with a 134 c.i., four-cylinder, L-head engine, and two-speed transmission, selling for $495. With optional electric starting, the price jumped to $550.

Roadside attractions

In nearby Salem, Indiana's oldest 1/2 mile race track, which opened in 1946, is still operating.
812-883-6504, call for schedule

New Castle

When Maxwell-Briscoe (predecessor of Chrysler Corporation) built its New Castle plant in 1906, it was the largest automobile plant in the nation. The company's opposed two-cylinder runabout sold for $750. By the summer of 1909, 9,000 Maxwells were sold. In 1909 the company became part of the United States Motor Company, which later collapsed in 1912. Four-cylinder versions followed with the Model D. In 1913 Maxwell salvaged what was left and continued to make inexpensive four-cylinder autos. Total production of cars and trucks at all plants in 1917 topped the 100,000 mark.

Walter P. Chrysler took over control of Maxwell and Chalmers, its associated company, in 1923. The Chrysler Six, introduced in 1924, outsold Maxwell's four-cylinder autos. The 1925 Maxwells were the last, to be replaced by the Chrysler four-cylinder car.

Chrysler has enjoyed a long association with the New Castle community. Today the facility at 18171 I Avenue manufactures auto and truck parts. The Dana Corporation - Spicer Axle Division plant produces castings, transmission cases and differential carriers, and Nuturn Corporation makes automotive brake blocks and linings.

Roadside attractions

Trump's Texaco Museum is located in a former gasoline station and displays related memorabilia including Texaco pumps and globes.
corner of of Brewer and Washington streets
765-345-7135, call for appointment

A Maxwell automobile is on display at the Wilbur Wright Birthplace & Museum in nearby Millville.
on Wilbur Wright Road, 765-332-2495
Hours: April through October
Monday through Saturday, 10 a.m. to 5 p.m.; Sunday, 1-5 p.m.

North Manchester

In 1908, a committee of local leaders campaigned to attract a new industry to the town. On July 5, 1908, the North Manchester Industrial Association signed a contract with Virgil L. DeWitt. It

continued on page 62

Behind the wheel

Today only one original DeWitt is known to exist. However, The DeWitt Motor Company resumed production in 1973 when Russell Egolf constructed a replica DeWitt for a local parade. This first replica was donated to the local historical society. Although Egolf was eager to produce more, he wanted to build them to impeccable standards. Eight years later he joined forces with Steve Farringer, and the pair began building "the only replica high-wheeled autos in the world," according to company material.

* * * * * *

Keck Motor Company in Mount Vernon, Indiana, claims the honor of being the oldest continuously operating Ford dealership in Indiana and among about the 20 oldest in the United States. It started when local businessman John Keck bought an automobile in 1903. He was so excited by it that he started an automobile division of Keck Gonnerman in 1907. In its early history, Keck handled many car lines such as Oakland, General, Packard, Studebaker and Cadillac, adding Ford in 1912. Keck started representing Ford exclusively in 1916.

It is still a family-owned business and is located on Highway 62 West.

* * * * * *

Every generation develops its own ways of communicating. The incrowd for the 1930's adopted "duesy," a part of the advertising slogan "It's a Duesy!"[TM] used to promote the luxury automobile, the Duesenberg. Although the spelling has been accepted in a variety of forms, "duesy" is used to express a kind of uncommon extravagance.

Today "It's a Duesy!" is a registered trademark and owned by the Auburn Cord Duesenberg Museum.

* * * * * *

provided that the association would turn over to DeWitt what was then known as the Eagle lot, lying west of the Big Four tracks, south of Main Street. In addition to this land, valued at $600, the association paid him $1,500. DeWitt built his automobile factory measuring not less than 35 x 125 feet, two stories high. DeWitt had been associated with the W.H. Kiblinger Company, later the W.H. McIntyre Company of Auburn. The DeWitt Motor Vehicle Company apparently built their vehicle under license from McIntyre.

The DeWitt Motor Buggy was a highwheeler with an air-cooled engine and solid rubber tires. DeWitt advertised "There is nothing cheap about the car but the price." Cars were manufactured between April 1909 and May 1910. It is believed that about 200 DeWitts were assembled before a fire put the company out of business. The building still exists.

Peru

In 1906, the Model Gas Engine Works moved to Peru from Auburn. In 1907, the company was divided into Model Gas Engine Works and the Model Automobile Company. The Model Automobile Company produced the Model (1906-1909) and the Star (1908). The Model was similar to the previous offering that was produced in Auburn. The Star was offered in two- or four-cylinder engine models. The Star Four was the most expensive at $4,000. In 1909, the automobile company was reorganized as the Great Western Automobile Company, and production continued in Peru under that name until 1914. The Great Western was built from 1909 to 1914.

Early Great Westerns were two-passenger roadsters and seven-passenger touring cars. In 1910 they introduced the Great Western Forty, so named for its 40-hp, four-cylinder engine. The Forty was offered in five models all available on a 114 in. wheelbase chassis. Great Western also custom-produced an auto called the Izzer in 1912 for a wealthy Chicago industrialist.

Did you know?
The 1932 Dusenberg SJ is considered by many auto experts today as one of the finest ever built.

Roadside attractions

The Miami County Museum has the 1955 Cadillac Fleetwood, once belonging to the world-famous songwriter and Indiana native Cole Porter. The original bill of sale and other historical documents relating to the car are also on display.
51 North Broadway, 765-473-9183
Hours: Tuesday through Saturday, 9 a.m. to 5 p.m.,
Sunday by appointment
closed Jan. 1, July 4, Thanksgiving and Christmas

In nearby Rochester, the Flagpole Drive-In has served old-fashioned home-made ice cream, sherbet, yogurt since 1949. Its patio-drive-thru is open March through October.
514 E. 9th Street, 219-223-6218
10 a.m. to 10 p.m.

Princeton

In 1995 Toyota chose Princeton for the location of its North American truck plant. Production of the 1999 full-size truck will commence in 1998. Employment is estimated at 1,300, with an initial capacity of 100,000 trucks.

Richmond

Of Richmond's 10 cars produced from 1901 to 1942, the Crosley, Davis and Westcott were the most well-known and respected. The Crosley is the exception that extended the auto manufacturing era here until the start of World War II. As in Muncie, automobile production in Richmond started with an auto named after the city.

The Richmond as well as the Wayne were built by Wayne Works. The Wayne Works also built school buses and early versions of what might today be called recreational vehicles. Its plant on the northwest corner of 16th Street and North F Street still exists today as part of the ICC Primex Plastics facility.

The Rodefeld Company built the Rodefeld touring car from 1909 to 1917. Rodefelds were built only after the company had the firm order in hand. Then, as now, a bigger part of their business consisted of repair parts. The company still exists at 96 West Main Street.

The Davis, was manufactured by the G.W. Davis Corporation from 1909 to 1928. The 1912 Davis was noted as the first car to use a center control gear shift and the Bendix self-starter. At the company's peak, it employed 1,000 and had cars in 26 foreign markets.

The Westcott Motor Car Company, successor to the Westcott Carriage Company, produced autos in Richmond from 1909 to 1916. Westcott is known for introducing the first front and rear bumpers as standard equipment in 1919 after they moved to Springfield, Ohio. An interesting note is that the carriage company employed Charles T. and Fred Fisher, two of the seven brothers who formed the Fisher Body Company. George Seidel, then manager of Wescott, remembered them as the "best carriage workers we ever had." After about a year, they left for Detroit in 1904. Fisher Body Company later became a division of General Motors.

Another Richmond manufacturer The Pilot Motor Car Company used the tagline "The Car Ahead." It was advertised as "Built to Wear--Not Just to Sell." Their 1914 advertisements described the "Pathfinder Tour" from Indianapolis to San Francisco, in which a Pilot 60 made the trip without any road adjustment. Claims like these were standard at the time.

The closing of Crosley Motors, Inc. in February 1942 for war production marked the end of auto manufacturing in Richmond. The plant exists today as Sanyo Corporation at 1751 Sheridan Street.

Today the automotive component market is alive and well in Richmond at Carpenter Manufacturing, Inc., and Dana Corporation. Carpenter manufactures school buses and passenger coaches. Dana's Richmond plants produce crankshafts, piston rings and cylinder liners.

Behind the wheel

Founder of piston-maker Perfect Circle, Ralph Teetor was inspired to invent cruise control while riding with his lawyer one day. The lawyer would slow down while talking and speed up while listening. The rocking motion so annoyed Teetor that he was determined to invent a speed control. The device made its debut in 1958 in the Chrysler Imperial, New Yorker and Windsor. Sidenote: Teetor had been blind since the age of five.

Roadside attractions

Wayne County Historical Museum houses a good collection of Richmond-made automobiles, including a 1909 Richmond, a 1918 Davis and a 1920 Pilot, as well as material related to the county's history.
1150 North A Street, 765-962-5756
Hours: February 4 through December 20
Tuesday through Friday, 9 a.m. to 4 p.m.
Saturday and Sunday, 1 to 4 p.m.

The 18-foot Madonna of the Trail honors pioneer women, who braved the National Road Trail in covered wagons, a precursor to early automotive travel. The monument is on U.S. 40 at the entrance of Glen Miller Park. The statue also commemorates Indiana's first tollgate on the National Road.

In nearby Cambridge City, The Huddleston Farmhouse Inn Museum is located on one of the most famous highways of U.S. history--U.S. Highway 40, also known as The National Road. This restored 1841 emigrant's house is designed to show visitors about the Huddleston's business of providing food and lodging during the heyday of travel along this route.
U.S. Hwy 40, one mile west of town, 765-478-3172
Hours: (February 5 to December 20) Tuesday through Saturday, 10 a.m. to 4 p.m.

In nearby Winchester, the Winchester Speedway is Indiana's second oldest race track and hold's the distinction of being the world's fastest half-mile track. USAC and NASCAR hold events here.
State Road 32 West, 765-584-9701
call for a schedule

In nearby Hagerstown, the Collectible Classics Car Museum features many unique cars in rotating displays, along with related memorabilia.
403 East Main Street, 765-489-5598
Winter hours: Thursday through Friday, 5-8 p.m.; Saturday, 1-6 p.m.
Summer hours: Monday through Saturday, 11 a.m. to 5 p.m.

Did you know?
Gaston Chevrolet's win in the 1920 Indianapolis 500, driving the Indianapolis-built Monroe, was the first win by an American car at the Brickyard since the National, also Indianapolis-built, won in 1912.

Ridgeville

In 1906, the Joseph Lay Company created a subsidiary, the Victor Automobile Company, to make two models of automobiles--the Senator and the Victor. Typical of most small-scale auto products in the era, these were assembled autos with most of the components ordered from various firms throughout the country.

The Senator was advertised as a touring car and sold for $2,000. It was built from 1907 to 1910 in a building adjacent to the Lay Broom and Brush Company. The Victor was listed as a roadster priced at $1,850 and was produced until about 1909. Total production may have been eight or nine vehicles. None are known to exist today, although the production supervisor's daughter is noted as having scavenged one of the brass Senator radiator grills.

South Bend

Automobile manufacturing in South Bend begins and ends with Studebaker. Studebaker is a key name in the area's annals of automobile production, but it's not by any means the only one. The majority of these other firms lasted only one or two years. Competition from the reigning town giant, Studebaker, may have discouraged others.

These other companies included: Perfection Auto Works (1907-1908), Tincher Motor Car Company (1907-1909), Ricketts Auto Works (1909), Diamond Auto Company produced the Diamond Arrow (1910-1911) the R.A.C. (1911-1912), Winkler Brothers Manufacturing Co. (1911-1912) and the South Bend Motor Works whose model was the South Bend (1913 - 1916).

The Studebaker saga begins with the founding of a small blacksmith shop in 1852 that later became the world's largest wagon manufacturer after the Civil War (more than 750,000 wagons, buggies, and carriages since 1852). Its automobile story begins with the sale of about 20 electric runabouts in 1902 and ends with the Avanti in 1963. The second electric car was sold to Thomas A. Edison. In those 61 years, Studebaker made the transition from wagon manufacturer to one of the largest auto manufacturers to the last independent auto producer in the United States.

The firm plunged into gasoline production after wetting its toes as agent for Garford (1904) and EMF (1908). Studebaker merged with and/or acquired both of these operations and production of electric cars was dropped on February 14, 1911, when the Studebaker Corporation was formed. Its abundant output has included luxury limousines; economy cars Erskine (1927-1930), Rockne (1932-1933)--named for Notre Dame's football coach--and the popular Champion first introduced in 1939; high performance Hawks and Avantis, and even racers that performed nobly at the Indianapolis 500 in 1932 and 1933; and trucks and military vehicles, notably the versatile World War II Weasel. Though armed with fresh designs, Studebaker couldn't stand up to the big three auto makers in the early 1960s. In December 1963, Studebaker's South Bend assembly lines closed.

The closing of production at the South Bend plants was greeted with much anger and disbelief. Today the city has weathered the storm and has a vibrant community.

Most all of the buildings from the Studebaker complex are intact. The administration building at the northwest corner of Bronson and South Main streets is now a training center for the local college.

Studebaker mileposts

1909/ Ranked fourth among American automobile producers.
1910
1911 Ranked second only to Ford.
1912- Ranked third after Ford and Willys-Overland.
1914
1913 Introduced a six-cylinder engine featuring monobloc engine casting (concurrent introduction along with Premier).
1915 Dropped to sixth place.
1921 Ranked fourth place after Ford, Buick and Dodge, and remained among the top 10 American producers through the 1920s.
1928 Set 160 endurance or speed records.
1931 Introduced free-wheeling.
1940 Survived the Depression.
1946 Introduced the 1947 Champion designed by Virgil Exner and became the largest independent automobile producer in the post-World War II period.
1949 One of the sole independents to develop its own automatic transmission while working with Borg-Warner of Muncie.
1963 Introduced the Avanti personal luxury car.

Roadside attractions

The Studebaker National Museum covers 114 years of its namesake's history. Studebaker helped shape America's industrial age by producing rugged covered wagons, carriages, automobiles and trucks, "the only company to span the time from settlers' wagons to high performance automobiles," according to museum material. The museum features the Studebaker family's own Conestoga wagon, used to move them to South Bend, and an Avanti, the last car made in South Bend. The carriage that Abraham Lincoln rode to Ford Theatre on night of his assassination is also on display.
525 S. Main Street, 219-235-9714
Hours: Monday through Saturday, 9 a.m. to 5 p.m.; Sunday, noon to 5 p.m.
closed on Thanksgiving and Christmas

Tippecanoe Place, the Studebaker mansion built in 1888, is now a fine dining restaurant with a casual ambiance. The mansion, with four main levels, 40 rooms and 20 fireplaces, illustrates the great wealth of the Studebakers.
620 W. Washington Street, 219-234-9077
Hours: 11:30 a.m. to 2 p.m. and 5 to 10 p.m. on weekdays (closing on Friday at 11 p.m.); Saturday, 4:30 to 11 p.m.;
Sunday, 9 a.m. to 2 p.m. and 4 to 9 p.m.

The Northern Indiana Center for History uses audiotapes, artifacts and photographs to recreate St. Joseph Valley's history, of which automobile manufacturing played a large role. (The Studebaker museum, however, covers automobile manufacturing in the area in greater depth.)
808 W. Washington Street, 219-235-9664
Hours: Tuesday through Saturday, 10 a.m. to 5 p.m.;
Sunday, noon to 5 p.m.
closed holidays

The former 840-acre Studebaker Proving Ground is 15 miles west of South Bend off State Route 2. The track is used by Bosch Braking Systems, and many acres are now the Bendix Woods County Park. Built in 1926, the "Million Dollar Outdoor Testing Lab" employed over 100 people and included a three-mile banked oval race track. A unique feature was the half-mile stand of pine trees at the north end of the track planted in 1937, spelling STUDEBAKER. The sign is formed by 8,200 trees with each letter 200 feet in length. It is reputed to be the largest arboreal sign in the world.

Behind the wheel

Work at the Studebaker plant was interwoven into the fabric of life in South Bend as evidenced by this account in *Studebaker: Less Than They Promised* by Michael Beatty.

"By 1900 South Bend was a bustling city of 36,000 residents, one out of every four born in a foreign country mostly from eastern Europe. South Bend was never a one-company town. Nevertheless, Studebaker was the largest employer, and many hundreds of Polish and Hungarian workers lived in neighborhoods to the west and southwest of downtown South Bend, where their small but well-kept homes were located within the sound of the factory's steam whistle which called them to work early in the morning and signaled lunch time and the end of the ten-hour work day.

"Many sons followed their fathers into the bustling factories, while their daughters often worked in the clothing plants which were located in South Bend because there was an ample supply of female labor. The census of 1920 showed that the booming city of South Bend had almost doubled its population in 20 years, to 71,000. Almost one out of every five residents was born outside the United States, and the proportion of immigrants among industrial workers was even greater."

* * * * * *

To save Studebaker from impending disaster, President Sherwood Egbert devised a plan in 1961 to save the company with a dramatically different car. He hired renowed industrial designer Raymond Loewy, who was responsible for the design of the Coca-Cola bottle, to create the Avanti. Loewy and his team of designers created a car with smooth curves and a narrow-waisted "Coke-bottle" shape.

The Avanti created a sensation at its unveiling April 1962. Studebaker, however, encountered production difficulties and couldn't meet consumer demand.

Studebaker closed in December 1963.

Terre Haute

A significant auto maker started its company in Terre Haute. The first Overland automobile was built at the Standard Wheel Works at 13th and Plum streets in 1902. The Wheel Works was the largest manufacturer of wheels in the world at the time with three plants in Ohio, one in Michigan, Fort Wayne, and Indianapolis, with the general offices in Terre Haute. The Terre Haute facility specialized in heavy wheels for wagons and trucks.

Claude E. Cox designed the Overland while he was a student at Rose Polytechnic Institute near Terre Haute. He worked at the Wheel Works as a wheel salesman while he was a student at the nearby college. His design had several innovations and received an unusual amount of attention. Cox placed the engine of his car in front remarking that it was the "logical" place for it. Cox also improved the seating arrangement by making the entrance to the rear seat compartment through the sides rather than through the rear of the auto as in earlier models.

The second story of one of the new buildings at the Wheel Works was devoted to manufacturing Overlands. Demand for the autos increased to the point that it was difficult to produce the necessary quantity at the Terre Haute facility. In 1905 Overland operations were moved to Indianapolis.

Cox continued to be affiliated with the automobile industry all of his life. In 1909 he left Indianapolis and joined the Interstate Automobile Company in Muncie. In two years he left Muncie for the Wilcox Motor Car Co. in Minneapolis. Then, in 1912, he became the Director of Research for General Motors Co. in Detroit. At the time of his death in 1964, Cox was president of Bartlett Research, Inc., an automotive research firm in Detroit.

With the departure of Overland, Terre Haute lost its sole direct link to the auto industry.

Roadside attractions

In nearby Perrysville, the Skinner Farm Museum is a privately owned, working farm. The owner has several vintage automobiles, tractors and farm equipment for viewing by appointment.
765-793-4079, call for appointment

Behind the wheel

The October 1960 issue of *Antique Automobile* and the *Encyclopedia Britannica* credited Lambert with building America's first successful automobile in 1891 while he was a resident of Ohio City, Ohio (a few miles across the state line, southeast of Decatur, Indiana). This predated both the Duryea (1893) and Haynes (1894) claims of building the first American auto.

Lambert may not have pressed his claim because he felt that although extremely successful mechanically, it was a financial failure because he was unable to generate sufficient sales to build it.

In 1902, Lambert formed the Union Auto Company in Union City to produce a rear-engine automobile with the gearless, friction-drive. (*See the Union Auto discussion in the Union City section for more detail on this auto.*) Then in 1905, Lambert formed Lambert Automobile, a division of Buckeye Manufacturing Company, in Anderson, which operated for 12 years, and closed the Union City facilities.

Lambert used his own specifications to design and build automobiles, trucks, fire engines, and farm tractors. All vehicles used the now proven friction-drive pioneered by Lambert.

By 1910, the Buckeye Company had over a thousand employees and production had reached 3,000 cars and trucks a year. During World War I, the Buckeye factories were converted for national defense use. At the conclusion of the war, Lambert correctly prophesied that a medium-sized, independent manufacturer would have to expand to a tremendous degree or eventually be merged with one of the large companies capable of mass production. Lambert chose to go into associated fields of automobile manufacturing.

Today only a few Lambert cars exist.

Union City

Union City, straddling the Ohio state line in Randolph County, once shared its name with two automotive businesses--the Union Automobile Company and Union City Body Company, Inc. Both of these entities have historic significance.

Union Automobile Company was formed in 1902 by John W. Lambert of Anderson to produce his rear-engine automobile with a gearless, friction-drive. Production was designed for 10 cars a month. One source lists over 300 Union cars were sold, none of which are know to exist today. The early Union was a two- or four-passenger auto. A front seat over the axle was accessible for the other two passengers by folding down the cover, which became the floorboard. Another unique feature of the Union was that it was guaranteed for one year from the purchase date. (Editorial comment: So much for today's extended warrantees.) The car sold for $1250 without extras. A $100 down payment was required with the balance due upon delivery. In 1905, Lambert formed Lambert Automobile, a division of Buckeye Manufacturing Company, in Anderson, and the Union Automobile Company was closed. (See sidebar.) The Union Auto building is currently used as a storage facility for the Sheller-Globe Corporation, which manufactures plastic and zinc automotive parts.

Union City businessmen C.C. Adelsperger, S.R. Bell, and J.W. Wogoman formed Union City Body Company to manufacture bodies for the horseless carriage in 1898. Early manufacturing was done principally for customers located within a radius of 100 miles. The company produced bodies for automotive pioneers Haynes, Apperson, Clark, Davis, H.C.S., Lexington, National, Premier, and Chandler. Later UCBC built bodies for some great names in the American automotive past such as Duesenberg, Cord, Essex, Pierce-Arrow, and the Auburn Speedster. The company manufactured these bodies until the decline of specialty automobiles in the late 1920s.

In the 1930s the company began the production of school bus bodies for various chassis manufacturers and truck cabs for Studebaker. During World War II, transit busses built on a Ford chassis were the sole products. In the 1950s, truck bodies were produced for installation on Ford, Dodge, GMC, and Chevrolet models until 1957 when an exclusive agreement was signed with Chevrolet and GMC Truck & Coach division.

Today at the 1015 West Pearl Street plant, the UCBC builds four delivery truck models with 64 different sizes and a medium duty van in 14 different body sizes. Customers include Frito-Lay, UPS, U.S. Postal Service and Federal Express. UCBC has manufactured over 390,800 bodies since their first walk-in van was introduced.

(Sidenote: Union City was also the birthplace of auto pioneer Harry C. Stutz, born 1876.)

Wabash

The Champion Auto Equipment Company made the Champion from 1916 to 1917. It was a two-passenger roadster with 183 c.i., four-cylinder, L-head engine.

Did you know?

Cruise In's continue throughout Indiana towns, although mostly in summer months. Here are a few sponsors along with information on how to contact them.

- Piston Poppers and Rax Restaurant in Anderson, 765-640-8142
- Miller's Drive-in in Rushville, 765-932-3062
- McDonalds on West National Road in Richmond, (call Marty Nolte for information) 765-966-9330
- Bill's Family Restaurant near New Castle, 765-529-9556

Events Calendar

The dates given below are the usually scheduled times for these events. We suggest that you contact the local convention bureaus listed at the end of this section to pinpoint actual dates and times. The Cruise-IN web site will also provide as much up-to-date information as possible. The address is www.cruise-in.com/resource/cruisein.htm

April

Fourth weekend, **Muncie**, Spring Auto Fair Swap Meet, Toy Show & Car Show at Delaware County Fairgrounds. Custom and antique cars on display.

May

Entire month, **Indianapolis**, Indianapolis 500 Festival, including exhibit at the Indianapolis Motor Speedway Hall of Fame Museum.

Third Saturday, **Indianapolis**, Spring Hoosier Auto Show Swap Meet

Friday and Saturday before Memorial Day, **Indianapolis**, The World's Largest Auto Racing Memorabilia show

Sunday before Memorial Day, **Indianapolis**, Indianapolis 500 Mile Race

Third weekend, **Terre Haute**, MDA Spring Fling Car Show & Cruise-In at Fairbanks Park. A two-day display of custom, classic, and antique vehicles.

Third weekend, **Nashville**, Indiana Shelby Spring Fling. The event features a jurored car show and road tour.

Third Weekend, **Lynn**, Community Days Car Show.

Third week, **Anderson**, Little 500 Festival & Race, Week-long celebration antique car show & Little 500 sprint car race on Saturday of Memorial Day weekend.

Saturday before Memorial Day, **Crown Point**, Cobe Cup Celebration. The rally commemorates one of the original road races, and only pre-1979 era cars, trucks and motorcycles are allowed.

Memorial Day weekend, Sunday, **Laporte**, Car Show & Swap Meet at Laporte County Fairgrounds. Antique and collector car show also includes an auto swap meet.

Memorial Day weekend, **Syracuse**, Friday & Saturday, Cruisin'Cuse Rod & Custom Car Show at Lakeland Youth Center. Antique & collector car show.

Memorial Day weekend, **Scottsburg**, Scott County Car Club Courtfest on the downtown square. Featuring antique & custom cars & trucks.

June

First weekend, **Crown Point**, Annual Rod & Custom Car Show & Swap Meet at Lake County Fairgrounds. The name says it all.

First weekend, **Loogootee**, Park & Spark Car Show at West Boggs Park. Car show and cruise-in featuring antique cars, street rods, pickups, and four-wheelers.

First weekend, **New Haven**, New Haven Canal Days - Downtown. Celebration includes car show and cruise-in.

First weekend, **Mentone**, Mentone Egg Festival, Downtown & Menser Park. Festival includes an antique car show.

First weekend, **Merom**, Merom Bluff Chautauqua at Merom Bluff Park. Events for everyone including classic cars, trucks and tractors.

First weekend, **Monon**, Monon Foodfest - Downtown. Festival includes a large car show.

Second weekend, **Evansville**, Classic Iron at the 4-H Center. Show with many displays including a car show.

Second weekend, **Mount Summit**, Summit Daze, Corner Prairie Road & School Street. Festival includes a car show.

Second Saturday, **Rockville**, Main Street Cruise-In & Street Dance on the town square. Open car show for all collectible vehicles, cars and tunes from the 50s.

Second Saturday, **Decatur**, The Decatur Police Reserves' Annual Car Show. Proceeds benefit local police reserves.

Second Sunday, **Liberty**, Antique and Classic Car Show at Whitewater Memorial State Park. See 22 classes of antique & classic cars.

Third weekend, **Gas City**, Jubilee Daze at Gas City Park. Cars from the 50s, 60s and 70s.

Third weekend, **Mulberry**, Homecoming Festival at Mulberry Park. Festival includes a car show.

Third Saturday, **Silver Lake**, Silver Lake Days Festival - various locations. Festival includes a car show.

Third Saturday, **Bridgeton**, Classic/Antique Car Show - various locations. Display of classic and antique cars.

Third Sunday, **Wanamaker**, Old Settlers Day on Southeastern Ave. Festival includes a car show.

Fourth week, **South Bend**, International Avanti Meet - various locations. See preserved and restored Avanti models.

Fourth weekend, **Marion**, "Cruisin" in the Park. A celebration for America's love affair with cars that includes a cruise through the city.

Fourth Sunday, **Indianapolis,** Concours d'Elegance. 200+ of the finest automobiles on display.

July

July 4th, **Danville**, Fun Feast-ival at Ellis Park. A feast for all senses, including antique and classic cars and antique tractors.

July 4, **Rushville**, 4th of July Car Show & Swap Meet in N. Memorial Park.

Weekend of or preceding July 4, **Etna Green**, Independence Events at Heritage Park. Events include a car show.

Weekend of or preceding July 4, **Kokomo**, Haynes - Apperson Festival on the courthouse square. Celebrates the city's automotive heritage.

Weekend of or preceding July 4, **Wabash**, Annual Honeywell Center Car Show. Visitors can look at more than 200 antique, classic, and street rod autos.

Weekend of or preceding July 4, **Salamonie**, Summer Festival - Downtown. Festival includes a classic car show.

July 4, **Wolcott**, Summer Festival at the Historic Wolcott House. Various events include antique car and truck show.

Second Saturday, **Richmond**, Wayne Co. 4-H Fair Car Show.

Second Sunday (1997 marks the first meet), **Rising Sun**, Annual Car Show. The event is tied to the town's Sounds of Summer concert series.

Third weekend, **Columbus**, Scottish Festival at Mill Race Park. The festival includes a British car show.

Third weekend, **Logansport**, Iron Horse Festival - Downtown. The transportation festival includes an auto show.

Third weekend, **Anderson**, Annual Indiana Vehicle Rally & Reunion, Military Armor Museum. the coordinators try to time the event with other activities in the area.

Third Sunday, **Rockville**, Early Wheels Antique and Classic Car Show at Billie Creek Village. Over 100 antique and classic cars on display.

Fourth weekend, **Battle Ground**, Battle Ground Steam & Gas Power Show at Tippecanoe Memorial Battlefield. The Gas Power Show includes antique cars and tractors.

Fourth weekend, **Berne**, Berne Swiss Days - various locations. Events for everyone, including a car show.

Fourth weekend, **Orland**, Vermont Settlement Festival at Town Park. The Settlement Festival includes a large car show.

Last week, **Lafayette**, Hot Summer Nights Festival - various locations. A sock-hoppin' hot spot with a classic car cruise-in and car show.

August

First weekend, **Indianapolis**, Brickyard 400 Festival. Several events precede the NASCAR race.

Second Friday, **North Manchester**, The Cruiz-in Illusions Cruise In. Display and judging of classic and special interestcars, hot rods, trucks and motorcycles.

Second Saturday, **Columbia City**, Classic Cruise-in on the courthouse square.

Second Sunday, **Laporte**, Annual Car Show & Swap Meet at the Laporte County Fairgrounds. The name says it all.

Second weekend, **Fort Wayne**, Muddy River Run at the Allen Country Fairgrounds. Over 1,800 classic cars--all pre-1958 models.

Third weekend, Sunday, **Bourbon**, Summerfest at Town Park. A street fair complete with a car show.

Fourth Saturday, **Centerville**, The Archway Festival Car Show. Several different catagories are open for judging.

Fourth weekend, **Selma**, Bluebird Festival at the Lions Club Building. Town carnival with a car show.

Fourth weekend, **Kentland**, Kentland Days on the court house square. Historical focus with antique auto and tractor show.

Fourth weekend, **Evansville**, Evansville Iron Street Rod Frog Follies at the Vanderburgh County 4-H Center. Car show and swap meet featuring hot rods galore.

Fourth weekend, **Knox**, Harvest Day Festival on the court house square. Festival includes a car show.

Fourth Saturday, **Rossville**, Rossville Summer's End Festival - Downtown. This farewell to summer includes a car show.

Fourth weekend, **Spencer**, Antique Car & Steam Train Festival - Downtown. Antique car display.

Fourth weekend, **Warsaw**, Custom Car & Truck Show. Display and judging of about 350 classic cars and trucks.

Last Sunday, **Turkey Run State Park**, Turkey Run Inn Annual "Cruise-In" & Classic Car Show.

Last weekend, **Winchester**, World Stock Car Festival.

September

Labor Day weekend, **Auburn**, The Auburn - Cord - Duesenberg Festival - various locations. Activities highlight the town's automotive legacy including the "Parade of Classics" and viewing of the A-C-D Club cars parked around the court house square on Saturday afternoon. Other must visits are the internationally acclaimed classic car museums and the Kruse collector car auction.

Labor Day weekend, **Boonville**, Labor Day Celebration at Warrick County 4-H Center. One of the state's oldest Labor Day celebrations includes a car show.

Labor Day weekend, **Ligonier**, Ligonier Marshmallow Festival on Main Street. Numerous activities include a car show.

Labor Day weekend, **Plymouth**, Marshall County Blueberry Festival at Centennial. Many activities with an antique car show.

Labor Day weekend, Sunday, **Clinton**, Festival of Ferrari's - 1803 East/1780 South. Come see the sleekest, sportiest, and fastest cars around.

Labor Day weekend, **Upland**, Labor Day Weekend Car Show. Car competition, with proceeds benefitting a deserving local person or family.

First weekend, Saturday, **Marshall,** Cruise-In & Classic Car Show at Turkey Run State Park. A full day of hot rods, classics and oldies.

First weekend, Sunday, **Petersburg,** Pike County Old Tyme Auto Show at Harnady Park. The show includes 16 classes of autos.

First (or second) weekend, **Nashville**, Annual Cider Run. Event includes a car show.

Second Sunday, **Elkhart**, Auto Fest, S. Ray Miller Auto Museum. Cars, trucks and custom or street rods can be entered into competition or just for display.

Third Sunday, **Burlington**, Burlington Fall Festival at Community Park. Festival includes a car show.

Third weekend, **Francesville,** Francesville Fall Festival - Downtwon. Festival includes an auto show.

Third weekend, **Indianapolis**, Hoosier Auto Show & Swap Meet at Marion County Fairgrounds. Antique, collector, and custom car show also includes one of the midwest's largest auto swap meets.

Last week, **Mitchell,** Annual Persimmon Festival on Main Street. An antique auto show is part of the events.

Fourth weekend, **Fairmount**, Fairmount Museum Days/Remembering James Dean Festival at Playacres Park. Includes a car show featuring cars of the James Dean Era.

Fourth weekend, Saturday, **Lewisville,** Stoplight Festival at the only stop light in town. Events include a car show.

Fourth weekend, **Muncie,** Rebel Run Car Show & Swap Meet at Delaware County Fairgrounds. Custom and antique display with automotive swap meet.

Fourth weekend, **Richland,** Richland Fest at Lions Park. The Festival includes a car show.

Fourth weekend, **Gas City**, Ducktail Run Road & Custom Show. Car competition and swap meet.

October

First weekend, **Bluffton,** Midwest Nostalgia Festival at Wells County 4-H Fairgrounds. 50s and 60s fun includes a car show.

First weekend, **Newport,** Newport Antique Auto Hill Climb. An uphill drag race for antique autos, plus collector car auction, car show and cruise-in.

First weekend, **Terre Haute,** Great Midwest Racing Weekend at the Wabash Valley Fairgrounds. Motorsports display with all kinds of race cars and a two-day racing show at the Action Track.

Second weekend, **Bainbridge,** Fall Festival. Activities include a car show.

Second weekend, **Plymouth,** Crossroads Cruise at Centennial Park. A unique auto event to commemorate the Transcontinental Highway including an auto cruise.

Second weekend, **Knightsville,** Knightsville Car Show at the Community House. Cars and trucks of all types and vintages are on exhibit.

Third Sunday, **Corydon,** Antique Auto Fest. All 1971 and older, unmodified cars, trucks and motorcycles are on display in the center of Indiana's first state capitol.

Indiana Convention and Visitors Bureaus:

Anderson/Madison County CVB, Anderson, 800-533-6569
Bloomington/Monroe County CVB, Bloomington, 800-800-0037
Clark/Floyd Counties CVB, Jeffersonville, 800-552-3842
Columbus Area Visitors Center, Columbus, 800-468-6564
Daviess County Visitors Bureau, Washington, 800-449-5262
Dearborn County CVB, Lawrenceburg, 800-322-8198
Dubois County Tourism Comm., Jasper, 800-238-3688
Elkhart County CVB, Elkhart, 800-262-8161
Evansville CVB, Evansville, 800-433-3025
Fort Wayne/Allen County CVB, Fort Wayne, 800-767-7752
Greater Lafayette CVB, Lafayette, 800-872-6648
Hamilton County CVB, Fishers, 800-776-8687
Henry County CVB, New Castle, 800-676-4302
Huntington County CVB, Huntington, 800-848-4282
Indianapolis CVA, Indianapolis, 800-323-4639
Jennings County Visitors Ctr.,Vernon, 800-928-3667
Kokomo/Howard County CVB, Kokomo, 800-837-0971
Kosciusko County CVB, Warsaw, 800-800-6090
LaGrange County CVB, LaGrange, 800-254-8090
Lake County CVB, Merrillville, 800-255-5253
LaPorte County CVB, Michigan City, 800-634-2650
Lawrence County Tourism Comm., Bedford, 800-798-0769
Madison Area CVB, Madison, 812-265-2956
Marion/Grant County CVB, Marion, 800-662-9474
Marshall County VCA, Plymouth, 800-626-5353
Montgomery County CVB, Crawfordsville, 800-866-3973
Muncie CVB, Muncie, 800-568-6862
Nashville/Brown County CVB, Nashville, 800-753-3255
Parke County CVB, Rockville, 765-569-5226
Porter County CVB, Chesterton, 800-283-8687
Putnam County CVB, Greencastle, 800-653-8687
Randolph County CVB, Winchester, 765-584-3622
Rising Sun/Ohio County CTVB, Rising Sun, 812-438-4933
South Bend/Mishawaka CVB, South Bend, 800-828-7881
Spencer County Tourism Comm., Santa Claus, 800-467-2682x209
Steuben County Tourism Bureau, Angola, 800-525-3101
Switzerland County CVB, Vevay, 800-435-5688
Terre Haute CVB, Terre Haute, 800-366-3043
Vincennes/Knox County Tourism, Vincennes, 812-886-0400
Wabash County CVB, Wabash, 800-563-1169
Wayne County CTB, Richmond, 800-828-8414

An Invitation

We hope this book has provided lots of information about the Indiana connection to the automobile. Be sure to visit this book's companion Web site (see below). This Web site is designed and maintained as a resource for the material presented in this book. There you will find information to make this a living resource such as an updated events calendar, discussions regarding the automobile in Indiana, and any new information since this book was published. Any further questions you have can be directed to us at

9220 N. College Avenue, Indianapolis, IN 46240-1031
Phone: 317-844-6869
Fax: 317-844-0669
e-mail: horvath@cruise-in.com or dhorvath@compuserve.com
Web address: http://www.cruise-in.com/resource/cruisein.htm

We'd especially enjoy hearing your stories about the automobile in Indiana.

Sincerely,

Dennis E. Horvath and Terri Horvath

Appendixes

Mileposts in Indiana automotive history

Early 19th century   National Road, U.S. highway built. Begun in 1815 and completed in 1833, it was the most ambitious U.S. road-building project undertaken up to that time. When completed, it extended from Cumberland, MD, to St. Louis, MO, and was the great highway of western migration. The present U.S. Highway 40 follows its route closely.

1885   The world's first gas pump is invented by Sylvanus F. Bowser of Fort Wayne.

1891   Charles H. Black of Indianapolis garners the dubious distinction of having Indiana's first auto accident when he ran his German manufactured Benz automobile into downtown store windows.

1894   Elwood Haynes demonstrates one of the earliest American automobiles along Pumpkinvine Pike, on the outskirts of Kokomo.

1895   Elwood Haynes introduces the first use of aluminum alloy in an automobile in the Haynes-Apperson crankcase.

1896   The corrugated metal pipe culvert is invented by two Crawfordsville men Stanley Simpson, the town engineer, and James H. Watson, a sheet metal worker. Their patented pipe culvert has now become a common sight on highway construction projects around the world.

1900   Tom and Harry Warner, Abbott and J.C. Johnson, Col. William Hitchcock and Thomas Morgan found Warner Gear Company of Muncie. Warner Gear's first major contribution to the industry was the differential.

1902   The Marmon motorcar, designed by Indianapolis auto maker Howard C. Marmon, has an air-cooled overhead valve V-twin engine and a revolutionary lubrication system that uses a drilled crankshaft to keep its engine bearings lubricated with oil-fed under pressure by a gear pump. This is the earliest automotive application of a system that has long since become universal to internal combustion piston engine design.

1902   The first Studebaker motorcar, introduced in South Bend, is an electric car. Studebaker Bros. had produced more than 750,000 wagons, buggies, and carriages since 1852.

1902   The Overland has its engine in the front, and rear-seat entrances are through the sides rather than the rear.

1903   The Auburn motorcar, introduced by Auburn Automobile Co. of Auburn, is a single-cylinder runabout with solid tires and a steering tiller. Charles, Frank and Morris Eckhardt of Eckhardt Carriage Co. started the firm with $7,500 in capital.

1903   The Haynes-Apperson is designed with a tilting steering column to allow easy access for the driver or passenger upon entering or leaving the vehicle.

1903   Premier claims that the oak leaf on its radiator badge is the first use of an emblem as an automobile trademark.

1905   The Haynes Model L has a semi-automatic transmission.

1906   American Motors Company of Indianapolis develops the American Underslung car, one of the first examples of low-center-of-gravity engineering.

1906   Maxwell-Briscoe (predecessor of Chrysler Corporation) builds its plant in New Castle. It is the largest automobile plant in the nation.

1906   National Motor Vehicle Company introduces a six-cylinder model, one of the first in America.

1907   Willys-Overland Motors is established by auto dealer John North Willys who takes over control of Overland Automobile of Indianapolis and moves it in 1909 to the old Pope-Toledo plant at Toledo, Ohio.

1909   Carl G. Fisher, James A. Allison, Arthur C. Newby and Frank H. Wheeler pool $250,000 in capital to form the Indianapolis Motor Speedway Company and transform an Indianapolis west side farm into a two-and-a-half-mile oval that becomes synonymous with automobile racing. The Speedway is designed as an automotive testing ground for U.S. manufactured automobiles to establish American auto supremacy. After the August motorcycle and auto races, the macadam track is repaved with 3,200,000 ten-pound bricks.

1910   The Cole Model 30 Flyer is among the first autos to offer pneumatic tires on demountable rims.

1910   The Cole Motor Car Company provides the first presidential automobile to President William Howard Taft.

1911   The first Indianapolis 500 Mile motorcar race is held May 30. A Marmon Wasp averages 75 miles per hour to win. The Wasp employs streamlining via elongated front and rear sections and adds the innovation of a rearview mirror.

1911   The Reeves Octoauto of Columbus introduces the first automobile powered by a V-8 engine.

1911   Haynes Automobile Company is the first to equip an open car with a top, a windshield, head lamps and a speedometer as standard equipment.

1912   Stutz Motor Car Company is founded by Harry C. Stutz, who merges his Stutz Auto Parts with Ideal Motor Car.

1912   The Davis car is the first to have a center-control gear shift and the Bendix self-starter.

1913   On July 1, the Lincoln Highway Association is created with Henry B. Joy (president, Packard Motor Company) as president and Carl G. Fisher as vice president. The Lincoln Highway is conceived as America's first transcontinental highway.

1913   Premier and Studebaker (both Indiana-built autos) concurrently introduce a six-cylinder engine featuring monobloc engine casting.

1914   The Haynes is one of the first autos to offer the Vulcan Electric Gear Shift as standard equipment.

1914   The Stutz Bearcat is introduced with a design patterned on the White Squadron racing cars that won victories last year. Stutz also produces family cars, while the Bearcat provides lively competition for the Mercer made at Trenton, NJ.

1916   The Marmon 34 priced at $2,700 and up is introduced with a "scientific lightweight" engine of aluminum. Designed by Howard Marmon with his Hungarian-American engineer Fred Moskovics and Alanson P. Brush, its only cast-iron engine components are its cylinder sleeves and one-piece "firing head." Body, fenders, hood, transmission case, differential housing, clutch cone wheel, and radiator shell are all of aluminum.

1918   The Cole Aero-Eight introduces the use of balloon tires.

1919   Westcott Motor Car Company introduces front and rear bumpers as standard equipment.

1920   The Duesenberg brothers (Fred S. and August S.) set up shop at Indianapolis to make motorcars.

1921   The Lafayette introduces thermostatically-controlled radiator shutters.

1922   The Model A Duesenberg, introduced by Duesenberg Motor Distributing Co. of Indianapolis, is the first U.S. production motorcar with hydraulic brakes, the first with an overhead camshaft, and the first U.S. straight eight engine. Ninety-two of the luxury cars are sold, a number that will rise to 140 in 1923.

1924   Chicago executive E. L. (Erret Lobban) Cord, 30, joins Auburn Automobile, gives its unsold inventory of 700 cars some cosmetic touch-ups, nets $500,000, and breathes new life into the company which is now owned by Chicago financiers including William Wrigley, Jr., but producing only six cars per day. Cord will double sales in 1925, introduce a new model, outperform and undersell the competition, and become president of Auburn in 1926.

1926   Safety-glass windshields are installed as standard equipment on high-priced Stutz motorcar models.

1926   E. L. Cord's Auburn Automobile Co. acquires Duesenberg Automobile and Motor Co.

1926   Warner Gear Company of Muncie develops the standardized transmission. It could be mass produced at half the cost of specialty transmissions and is suitable for use in most automobiles.

1928   Studebaker sets 160 endurance or speed records.

1928   Auburn comes out with an 8-cylinder, 115-hp model advertised with a picture of 115 stampeding horses. Its boat-tailed speedster travels at 108.6 miles per hour at Daytona, FL, in March and later in the year averages 84.7 miles per hour for 25 hours at Atlantic City, NJ.

1929   The first motorcar (Cord L-29) with front-wheel drive is introduced by E. L. Cord's Auburn Automobile Company.

1929   The Model J Duesenberg introduced by E. L. Cord's Duesenberg, Inc., is a "real Duesy." The costly 265-hp luxury car can go up to 116 miles per hour and will be built until 1936.

1929   Marmon warrants a listing in the Guiness Book of Records for its factory-installed radio.

1929   The Roosevelt has the distinction of being the first eight-cylinder car in the world to sell for less than $1,000.

1931   In February, before production started, the Society of Automotive Engineers honored Colonel Howard Marmon for "the most notable engineering achievement of 1930," his huge and gleaming V-16 engine design. The society was especially impressed by his extensive use of lightweight aluminum, generally a difficult metal to work and maintain in automobile power plants.

1931   Studebaker introduces free-wheeling.

1931   Stutz introduces drop-side bodies, an American production first. These bodies had doors that dropped to the running boards and covered the frame rails completely. Within a few years, all American cars follow Stutz's lead; this drop-side body and sponsorship of Weymann construction are Stutz's great contributions to the advance of coachwork.

1931   Auburn motorcar sales soar to 34,228, and profits equal those of 1929 after a depressing 1930 sales year. E. L. Cord signs up 1,000 new dealers as his car climbs from 23rd place in retail sales to 13th on the strength of the new Auburn 8-98. The new Auburn is the first rear-drive motorcar with a frame braced by an X-cross member and the first moderately priced car with L.G.S. Free Wheeling.

1932   The first gasoline pump that could accurately measure dispensed gas and give the price in dollars and cents is introduced in Fort Wayne.

1932   Graham Brothers of Evansville introduces full-skirted fenders.

1932   The Duesenberg SJ is the first stock automobile to be equipped with a centrifugal type supercharger, although some have previously been fitted with Roots type blowers.

1932   The Stutz DV32 is one of the few American cars equipped with a four-speed transmission.

1932   William B. Barnes invents overdrive, a device that would increase the life of the engine, yet improve fuel efficiency. Muncie's Warner Gear backs the development.

1936   The Cord 810 introduced by Auburn Automobile Company is a sleek modern motorcar with advanced features that include disappearing headlights, concealed door hinges, rheostat-controlled instrument lights, variable speed windshield wipers, Bendix Electric Hand (steering column-mounted electric gear pre-selection unit), and is the first automobile in this country to adopt unit body construction in its full sense. (Chrysler-Airflow and Lincoln-Zepher used modified forms.)

1937   Studebaker is the first American car to offer windshield washers.

1947   Guide Lamp introduces plastic tail light lenses.

1958   Ralph Teetor, Perfect Circle Corporation president, invents cruise control, introduced on the Chrysler Imperial, New Yorker and Windsor models.

1964   Studebaker-Packard breaks with the majors and becomes the first U.S. maker to offer seat belts as standard equipment.

1984   The Hummer is introduced by AM General of Mishawaka. Originally intended as a military personnel carrier, the Hummer is now sold as an off-road (street-legal,) general-purpose, four-passenger vehicle

Primary resources

Anderson

Bailey, L. Scott, 1891 Lambert: A New Claim for America's First Gasoline Automobile, *Antique Automobile*, October 1960.

Dittlinger, Esther, *Anderson: A Pictorial History*, St. Louis, MO, G. Bradley Publishing Inc., C 1990

Auburn

Borgeson, Griffith, E. L. Cord: Biography, Princeton, NJ, *Automobile Quarterly Publications*, C 1984

Burger, Dan, Auburn Automobile Company, *Antique Automobile*, reprint

Kimes, Beverly Rae, *Standard Catalog of American Cars: 1805 - 1942*, Iola, WI, Krause Publications, C 1996

Smith, John Martin, *A History of DeKalb County Indiana 1837-1987*, C 1987

Columbus

Georgano, G. N., *The Complete Encyclopedia of Motorcars 1885 to the Present*, New York, NY, E. P. Dutton and Company Inc., C 1968

Leich, Alexander, Cars of Indiana, *Motor Trend*, September and October 1965

Connersville

Blommel, Henry, Connersville: The "Little Detroit of Indiana", *Antique Automobile*, March 1969

Blommel, Henry, Auburn and Cord in Connersville, *Cars & Parts*, May 1986

Smith, Harry M., *Connersville: A Pictorial History*, St. Louis, MO, G. Bradley Publishing Inc., C 1992

Walters, H. Max, *The Making of Connersville and Fayette County*, Baltimore, MD, Gateway Press, Inc., C 1988

Elkhart

Georgano, G. N., *The Complete Encyclopedia of Motorcars 1885 to the Present*, New York, NY, E. P. Dutton and Company Inc., C 1968

Hampton, Charles C., *The Automobile Industry in Elkhart*, monograph, C 1977

Riebs, George E., *Elkhart: A Pictorial History*, St. Louis, MO, G. Bradley Publishing Inc., C 1990

Evansville

Georgano, G. N., *The Complete Encyclopedia of Motorcars 1885 to the Present*, New York, NY, E. P. Dutton and Company Inc., C 1968

Leich, Alexander, Cars of Indiana, *Motor Trend*, September and October 1965

Indianapolis

Baker, David L., *Indianapolis-Marion County Automobile Industry*, Indianapolis, Indianapolis Historic Preservation Commission, c 1990

Butler, Don, *Auburn Cord Duesenberg*, Osceola, WI, Motorbooks International, C 1992

Carson, Richard B., *The Olympian Cars: The Great American Luxury Automobiles of the Twenties*, New York, NY, Alfred A. Knopf, C 1976

Delancy, Howard R., *History of the Cole Motor Car Company*, Bloomington, IN, D.B.A. dissertation, Indiana University., C 1954

Indianapolis continued

Elbert, J. L., *Duesenberg: the mightiest American motor car*, Arcadia, CA, Post Era Books, C 1951

Flink, James J., *The Automobile in American Culture*, Cambridge, MA, M.I.T. Press

Georgano, G. N., *The Complete Encyclopedia of Motorcars 1885 to the Present*, New York, NY, E. P. Dutton and Company Inc., C 1968

Hanley, George Philip, *The Marmon Heritage*, Rochester, MI, Doyle Hyk Publishing Co., C 1985

Horseless Carriage Club of Indianapolis, Yearbook, Indianapolis, IN, C 1950

Kimes, Beverly Rae, *Standard Catalog of American Cars: 1805 - 1942*, Iola, WI, Krause Publications, C 1996

Steinwedel, Louis W., *The Duesenberg*, New York, NY, Norton, C 1982

Kokomo

Booher, Ned, *Howard County: A Pictorial History*, Virginia Beach, VA, The Donning Co., C 1994

Booher, Ned, *Kokomo: A Pictorial History*, St. Louis, MO, G. Bradley Publishing Inc., C 1989

Gray, Ralph D., *Alloys and Automobiles: the Life of Elwood Haynes*, Indianapolis, IN, Indiana Historical Society, C 1979

Haynes, Elwood, *The Complete Motorist*, Kokomo, IN, The Haynes Automobile Co., C 1913 and Shearer Printing Inc., C 1977

Odiet, Fred C., *Kokomo-Howard County Sesquicentennial Commemorative Book*, Kokomo, IN, C 1994

Lafayette

Georgano, G. N., *The Complete Encyclopedia of Motorcars 1885 to the Present*, New York, NY, E. P. Dutton and Company Inc., C 1968

LaPorte

Georgano, G. N., *The Complete Encyclopedia of Motorcars 1885 to the Present*, New York, NY, E. P. Dutton and Company Inc., C 1968

Lawrenceberg

Lawrenceberg: A Pictorial History, St. Louis, MO, G. Bradley Publishing Inc., C 1990

Georgano, G. N., *The Complete Encyclopedia of Motorcars 1885 to the Present*, New York, NY, E. P. Dutton and Company Inc., C 1968

Kimes, Beverly Rae, *Standard Catalog of American Cars: 1805 - 1942*, Iola, WI, Krause Publications, C 1996

Ligonier

Mier Carriage and Buggy Company, catalog, 1908

Marion

Georgano, G. N., *The Complete Encyclopedia of Motorcars 1885 to the Present*, New York, NY, E. P. Dutton and Company Inc., C 1968

Mishawaka

Georgano, G. N., *The Complete Encyclopedia of Motorcars 1885 to the Present*, New York, NY, E. P. Dutton and Company Inc., C 1968

Kimes, Beverly Rae, *Standard Catalog of American Cars: 1805 - 1942*, Iola, WI, Krause Publications, C 1996

Muncie
Announce Plans of New Company, *The Muncie Star*, May 11, 1920
Georgano, G. N., *The Complete Encyclopedia of Motorcars 1885 to the Present*, New York, NY, E. P. Dutton and Company Inc., C 1968
Lemasters, Ron, Interstate Brought Muncie Into the Auto World in 1908, *The Muncie Star*, July 3, 1976.
Spurgeon, Wiley W. Jr., *Muncie & Delaware County: An Illustrated Retrospective*, Woodland Hills, CA, Windsor Publications, C 1984

New Albany
Georgano, G. N., *The Complete Encyclopedia of Motorcars 1885 to the Present*, New York, NY, E. P. Dutton and Company Inc., C 1968

New Castle
Georgano, G. N., *The Complete Encyclopedia of Motorcars 1885 to the Present*, New York, NY, E. P. Dutton and Company Inc., C 1968

North Manchester
DeWitt Motor Vehicle Company, marketing materials
Manifold, Orrin, *North Manchester's Automobile Factory*, North Manchester, IN, North Manchester Historical Society, May 1986

Peru
Georgano, G. N., *The Complete Encyclopedia of Motorcars 1885 to the Present*, New York, NY, E. P. Dutton and Company Inc., C 1968
Kimes, Beverly Rae, *Standard Catalog of American Cars: 1805 - 1942*, Iola, WI, Krause Publications, C 1996

Richmond
Peters, Sue, First Locally Built Car-The Richmond, *Palladium-Item*, July 3, 1988
Thompson, Frances, Pilot: The Car Ahead, *Tri-State Trader*, October 18, 1980
Tyndall, Bill, Teetor-Harley co-authored small-town success, *Palladium-Item*, August 14, 1994
Wayne County Historical Museum, Docent notes for the auto collection
Ward, Gertrude, *Richmond: A Pictorial History*, St. Louis, MO, G. Bradley Publishing Inc., C 1994

Ridgeville
Norton, Wayne L., *Yester Year Ridgeville*, monograph, C 1989

South Bend
Beatty, Michael, *Studebaker: Less that they Promised*, South Bend, IN, And Books, C 1984
Cannon, William A., *Studebaker: The Complete Story*, Blue Ridge Summit, PA, TAB Books, C 1981
Erskine, Albert Russel, *History of the Studebaker Corporation*, Chicago, IL, Poole Bros., C 1918
Flink, James J., *The Automobile Age*, Cambridge, MA, M.I.T. Press, C 1988
Hall, Asa E., *The Studebaker Century*, Contocock, NH, Dragonwyck Publishing, Inc., C 1983

Terre Haute
Calvert, Judy Stedman, First Overland Motor Car Built in Terre Haute, *Terre Haute Journal*, January 1, 1983
Jerse, Dorothy Weinz, *Terre Haute: A Pictorial History*, St. Louis, MO, G. Bradley Publishing Inc., C 1993

Union City
Bailey, L. Scott, 1891 Lambert: A New Claim for America's First Gasoline Automobile, *Antique Automobile*, October 1960
Union Automobile Company, marketing materials
Union City Body Company, marketing materials

Wabash
Georgano, G. N., *The Complete Encyclopedia of Motorcars 1885 to the Present*, New York, NY, E. P. Dutton and Company Inc., C 1968

Mileposts in Indiana automotive history
Dauphinais, Dean E., *Car Crazy: The Official Motor City High-Octane, Turbocharged, Chrome-Plated, Back Road Book of Car Culture*, Detroit, MI, Visible Ink Press, C 1996
Hanley, George Philip, *The Marmon Heritage*, Rochester, MI, Doyle Hyk Publishing Co., C 1985
Jordan, Ben, *Ben Jordan's Automotive Jargon for the Car Owner from the Shade Tree Mechanic's Automobile Dictionary with Lagniappe*, Denver, Co, Windmill Jouster Books, C 1995
Trager, James, *The People's Chronology*, Henry Holt and Company, C 1992

Indiana-built autos
Huffman, Wallace Spencer, *Indiana Built Motor Vehicles Centennial Edition*, Indianapolis, Indiana Historical Society, C 1994.
Kimes, Beverly Rae, *Standard Catalog of American Cars: 1805 - 1942*, Iola, WI, Krause Publications, C 1996

Bibliography

Bailey, L. Scott, 1891 Lambert: A New Claim for America's First Gasoline Automobile, *Antique Automobile*, October 1960.

Baker, David L., Indianapolis-Marion County Automobile Industry, Indianapolis, Indianapolis Historic Preservation Commission, c 1990

Beatty, Michael, *Studebaker: Less that they Promised*, South Bend, IN, And Books, C 1984

Blommel, Henry, Connersville: The "Little Detroit of Indiana", *Antique Automobile*, March 1969

Blommel, Henry, Auburn and Cord in Connersville, *Cars & Parts*, May 1986

Booher, Ned, *Howard County: A Pictorial History*, Virginia Beach, VA, The Donning Co., C 1994

Booher, Ned, *Kokomo: A Pictorial History*, St. Louis, MO, G. Bradley Publishing Inc., C 1989

Borgeson, Griffith, *E. L. Cord: Biography*, Princeton, NJ, Automobile Quarterly Publications, C 1984

Buehrig, Gordon M., The year 1936 is viewed fifty years later by Gordon Buehrig for the ACD Club 1986, Auburn, IN, C 1986

Burger, Dan, Auburn Automobile Company, *Antique Automobile*, reprint

Butler, Don, *Auburn Cord Duesenberg*, Osceola, WI, Motorbooks International, C 1992

Calvert, Judy Stedman, First Overland Motor Car Built in Terre Haute, *Terre Haute Journal*, January 1, 1983

Carson, Richard B., *The Olympian Cars: The Great American Luxury Automobiles of the Twenties*, New York, NY, Alfred A. Knopf, C 1976

Calder, J. Kent, *Traces: 100 Years of Automotive History*, Indianapolis, IN, Indiana Historical Society, Spring 1994

Cannon, William A., *Studebaker: The Complete Story*, Blue Ridge Summit, PA, TAB Books, C 1981

Darrell, James D., The Auburn Story: the classics come home, *The Auburn Evening Star: supplement for 17th ACD festival*, C 1972

Dauphinais, Dean E., *Car Crazy: The Official Motor City High-Octane, Turbocharged, Chrome-Plated, Back Road Book of Car Culture*, Detroit, MI, Visible Ink Press, C 1996

Delancy, Howard R., *History of the Cole Motor Car Company*, Bloomington, IN, D.B.A. dissertation, Indiana University., C 1954

DeWitt Motor Vehicle Company, marketing materials

Dittlinger, Esther, *Anderson: A Pictorial History*, St. Louis, MO, G. Bradley Publishing Inc., C 1990

Doolittle, James R., *Romance of the Automobile Industry*, New York, NY, Klebold Press, C 1916

Elbert, J. L., *Duesenberg: the mightiest American motor car*, Arcadia, CA, Post Era Books, C 1951

Erskine, Albert Russel, *History of the Studebaker Corporation*, Chicago, IL, Poole Bros., C 1918

Flink, James J., *America Adopts the Automobile, 1895 - 1910*, Cambridge, MA, M.I.T. Press, C 1970

Flink, James J., *The Car Culture*, Cambridge, MA, M.I.T. Press, C 1975

Flink, James J., *The Automobile Age*, Cambridge, MA, M.I.T. Press, C 1988

Flink, James J., *The Automobile in American Culture*, Cambridge, MA, M.I.T. Press

Forbes, Bernice Charles, *Automotive Giants of America*, New York, B.C. Forbes Publishing Co., C 1926

Gentry, Lorna, *Autos: Imagination, Invention & Industry*, Cincinnati, OH, Creative Company, C 1991

Georgano, G. N., *The Complete Encyclopedia of Motorcars 1885 to the Present*, New York, NY, E. P. Dutton and Company Inc., C 1968

Glasscock, Carl Burgess, *Motor History of America*, New York, NY, Bobbs-Merrill Co, C 1937 and C 1946

Gray, Ralph D., *Alloys and Automobiles: the Life of Elwood Haynes*, Indianapolis, IN, Indiana Historical Society, C 1979

Hall, Asa E., The Studebaker Century, Contocok, NH, Dragonwyck Publishing, Inc. C 1983

Hampton, Charles C., *The Automobile Industry in Elkhart*, monograph, C 1977

Hanley, George Philip, *The Marmon Heritage*, Rochester, MI, Doyle Hyk Publishing Co., C 1985

Haynes, Elwood, *The Complete Motorist*, Kokomo, IN, The Haynes Automobile Co., C 1913 and Shearer Printing Inc., C 1977

Hokanson, Drake, *The Lincoln Highway: Main Street Across America*, Iowa City, IA, University of Iowa Press, C 1988

Horseless Carriage Club of Indianapolis, Yearbook, Indianapolis, IN, C 1950

Huffman, Wallace Spencer, *Indiana Built Motor Vehicles Centennial Edition*, Indianapolis, Indiana Historical Society, C 1994.

Jerse, Dorothy Weinz, *Terre Haute: A Pictorial History*, St. Louis, MO, G. Bradley Publishing Inc., C 1993

Jordan, Ben, *Ben Jordan's Automotive Jargon for the Car Owner from the Shade Tree Mechanic's Automobile Dictionary with Lagniappe*, Denver, Co, Windmill Jouster Books, C 1995

Kimes, Beverly Rae, *Standard Catalog of American Cars: 1805 - 1942*, Iola, WI, Krause Publications, C 1996

Lemasters, Ron, Interstate Brought Muncie Into the Auto World in 1908, *The Muncie Star*, July 3, 1976.

Leich, Alexander, Cars of Indiana, *Motor Trend*, September and October 1965

Lincoln Highway Association, *The Complete Official Road Guide of the Lincoln Highway -- Fifth edition*, Detroit, C 1924, and The Patrice Press, Tucson, AZ, C 1993

Manifold, Orrin, *North Manchester's Automobile Factory*, North Manchester, IN, North Manchester Historical Society, May 1986

Odiet, Fred C., *Kokomo-Howard County Sesquicentennial Commemorative Book*, Kokomo, IN, C 19941

Mier Carriage and Buggy Company, catalog, 1908

Norton, Wayne L., *Yester Year Ridgeville*, monograph, C 1989

Peters, Sue, First Locally Built Car-The Richmond, *Palladium-Item*, July 3, 1988

Riebs, George E., *Elkhart: A Pictorial History*, St. Louis, MO, G. Bradley Publishing Inc., C 1990

Schlereth, Thomas J., *U.S. 40: A Roadscape of the American Experience*, Indianapolis, IN, Indiana Historical Society, C 1985

Smith, Harry M., *Connersville: A Pictorial History*, St. Louis, MO, G. Bradley Publishing Inc., C 1992

Smith, John Martin, *A History of DeKalb County Indiana 1837-1987*, C 1987

Spurgeon, Wiley W. Jr., *Muncie & Delaware County: An Illustrated Retrospective*, Woodland Hills, CA, Windsor Publications, C 1984

Steinwedel, Louis W., *The Duesenberg*, New York, NY, Norton, C 1982

Thompson, Frances, Pilot: "The Car Ahead", *Tri-State Trader*, October 18, 1980

Trager, James, *The People's Chronology*, Henry Holt and Company, C 1992

Tyndall, Bill, Teetor-Harley co-authored small-town success, *Palladium-Item*, August 14, 1994

Union Automobile Company, marketing materials

Union City Body Company, marketing materials

Walters, H. Max, *The Making of Connersville and Fayette County*, Baltimore, MD, Gateway Press, Inc., C 1988

Ward, Gertrude, *Richmond: A Pictorial History*, St. Louis, MO, G. Bradley Publishing Inc., C 1994

Wayne County Historical Museum, Docent notes for the auto collection

Weinhardt, Carl J., *An Investigation of the rise and fall of the automobile industry in Indiana*, B.A. thesis, Boston, MA, Harvard University., C 1948

Weintraut, Linda, *Losing the Business: How Hoosier Automobile Manufacturers Failed Middle America*, M.A. thesis, Indianapolis, Indiana University, C 1989

Indiana-built automobiles sorted by city

City	Name	Manufacturer	Date
Albany	Albany	Albany Automobile Co.	1907-08
Anderson	Anderson	Anderson Carriage Mfg. Co.	1907-10
	Anderson Steam	Anderson Steam Carriage Co.	1901-02
	De Tamble	De Tamble Motor Co.	1908-13
	Erie	Erie Cycle & Motor Carriage Co.	1899-1902
	Excellent Six	Rider-Lewis Motor Car Co.	1908-11
	Lambert	Buckeye Mfg. Co.	1906-17
	Laurel	Laurel Motors Corp.	1917-20
	Madison	Madison Motors Corp.	1915-19
	Nyberg	Nyberg Automobile Works	1911-13
	Rider-Lewis	Rider-Lewis Motor Car Co.	1908-11
	Union	Buckeye Mfg. Co.	1905
Auburn	Auburn	Auburn Automobile Co.	1900-36
	Auburn Motor Chassis	Auburn Motor Chassis Co.	1912-15
	Cord	Cord Corp.	1929-32
	De Soto	Zimmerman Mfg. Co.	1913-14
	Handy Wagon	Auburn Motor Chassis Co.	1912-15
	Imp	W. H. McIntyre Co.	1913-14
	Kiblinger	W. H. Kiblinger Co.	1907-08
	McIntyre	W. H. McIntyre Co.	1909-15
	McIntyre Special	W. H. McIntyre Co.	1911-15
	Model	Model Gas Engine Works	1903-06
	Union	Union Automobile Co.	1916
	Zimmerman	Zimmerman Mfg. Co.	1908-15
Bedford	Postal	Postal Automobile & Engineering Co.	1906-08
Butler	Butler High Wheel	Butler Co.	1908
Columbia City	Harper	Harper Buggy Co.	1907-08
Columbus	Reeves	Reeves Pulley Co.	1896-98, 1905
Connersville	Ansted	Lexington Motor Car Co.	1921, 1926
	Auburn	Auburn Automobile Co.	1929-36
	Cord	Cord Corp.	1936-37
	Empire	Empire Motor Car Co.	1912-15

	Howard	Lexington-Howard Co.	1913-14
	Lexington	Lexington Motor Co.	1910-27
	McFarlan	McFarlan Motor Car Co.	1910-28
	Packard Darrin	Packard Motor Car Co.	1940-41
	Pak-Age-Car	Auburn Automobile Co.	1938-41
	Van Auken Electric	Connersville Buggy Co.	1913
Decatur	Decatur	Decatur Motor Car Co.	1908-11
Elkhart	Allied	Allied Cab Mfg. Co.	1932-34
	Black Crow	Crow Motor Car Co.	1909-11
	Crow	Crow Motor Car Co.	1911
	Crow-Elkhart	Crow Motor Car Co.	1911-23
	El-Fay	Elkhart Motor Co.	1931-35
	Elcar	Elkhart Motor Co.	1916-31
	Huffman	Huffman Bros. Motor Co.	1920-25
	Komet	Elkhart Motor Car Co.	1911
	Martel	Elkhart Motor Co.	1925-27
	Morriss-London	Century Motors Co.	1919-25
	Niagara Four	Crow Motor Car Co.	1915-16
	Pratt	Pratt Motor Car Co.	1911-15
	Pratt-Elkhart	Elkhart Carriage & Harness Mfg. Co.	1909-11
	Prosperity	Allied Cab Mfg. Co.	1933
	Royal	Royal Motor Co.	1913
	Royal Martel	Elkhart Motor Co.	1925-27
	Shoemaker	Shoemaker Automobile Co.	1907-08
	Sterling	Elkhart Motor Car Co.	1909-11
	Sun	Sun Motor Car Co.	1916-17
	Super Allied	Allied Cab Mfg. Co.	1935
Evansville	Evansville	Evansville Automobile Co.	1907-09
	Graham-Paige	Graham-Paige	1929-30
	Muntz Jet	Muntz Car Co.	1950-51
	Plymouth	Chrysler Corp.	1935-56
	Simplicity	Evansville Automobile Co.	1907-11
	Single-Center	Single-Center Buggy Co.	1906-08
	Traveler	Traveler Automobile Co.	1910-11
Fort Wayne	Chevrolet Truck	General Motors Truck & Bus Group	1986-present
	Ideal-Commercial	Ideal Auto Co.	1910-14
	Scout	International Harvester Co.	1961-80
Frankfort	Bour-Davis	Shadburne Bros. Co.	1918
	Red Ball-Taxi	Red Ball Transit Co.	1924

Franklin	Martindale & Millikan	Indian Motor & Mfg. Co.	1914
	Continental	Indian Motor & Mfg. Co.	1910-13
Gary	Gary Six	Gary Automobile Mfg. Co.	1914
Greensburg	United	United Engineering Co.	1919-20
Huntingburg	Huntingburg	Huntingburg Wagon Works	1902-03
Indianapolis	American	American Motors Co.	1906-14
	American Underslung	American Motors Co.	1906-14
	Black	C.H. Black Mfg. Co.	1896-1900
	Blackhawk	Stutz Motor Car Co.	1929-30
	Brook Spacke	Machine & Tool Co.	1920-21
	Cole	Cole Motor Car Co.	1909-25
	Cole Solid Tire	Cole Carriage Co.	1908-09
	Comet	Comet Cyclecar Co.	1914
	Comet Racer	Marion Motor Car Co.	1904
	Cyclop	L. Porter Smith & Bros.	1910
	Duesenberg	Duesenberg Motors Corp.	1920-37
	Electrobile	National Vehicle Co.	1901-06
	Elgin	Elgin Motors Inc.	1923-24
	Empire	Empire Motor Car Co.	1909-19
	Ford	Ford Motor Co.	1914-32
	H.C.S.	H.C.S. Motor Co.	1920-25
	H.C.S. Cab	H.C.S. Cab Mfg. Co.	1924-27
	Henderson	Henderson Motor Car Co.	1912-14
	Herff-Brooks	Herff-Brooks Corp.	1915-16
	Hoosier Scout	Warren Electric & Machine Co.	1914
	Ideal	Ideal Motor Co.	1911-12
	Indiana	Indiana Motor & Vehicle Co.	1901
	Lafayette	Lafayette Motors Co.	1921-22
	Lindsay	T.J. Lindsay Automobile Parts Co.	1902-03
	Lyons-Knight	Lyons-Atlas Co.	1913-15
	Mais	Mais Motor Truck Co.	1911-14
	Marathon	Herff-Brooks Corp.	1915-16
	Marion	Marion Motor Car Co.	1904-14
	Marmon	Nordyke & Marmon Co.	1902-33
	McGill	McGee Mfg. Co.	1917-28
	Merz	Merz Cyclecar Co.	1914
	Mohawk	Mohawk Cycle & Automobile Co.	1903-05

	Monroe	William Small Co.	1918-23
	National	National Motor Vehicle Co.	1904-24
	National Electric	National Automobile & Electric Co.	1900-04
	New Parry	Parry Auto Co.	1911-12
	Overland	Standard Wheel Works	1905-06
	Overland	Overland Auto Co.	1906-09
	Pak-Age-Car	Stutz Motor Co.	1930-38
	Parry	Parry Auto Co.	1910
	Pathfinder	Motor Car Mfg. Co.	1912-17
	Pope-Waverly	Pope Motor Car Co.	1904-08
	Premier	Premier Motor Mfg. Co.	1903-26
	Premier Taxicab	Premier Motor Car Co.	1923-26
	Roosevelt	Marmon Motor Car Co.	1929-30
	Spacke	Spacke Machine & Tool Co.	1919
	Stutz	Stutz Motor Car Co.	1912-35
	Tricolet	H. Pokorney & Richards Auto./Gas.	1904-06
	Waverly	Waverly Co.	1909-16
	Waverly Electric	Indiana Bicycle Co.	1898-1903
Knightstown	Leader	Leader Mfg. Co.	1907-12
Kokomo	Apperson	Apperson Bros. Automobile Co.	1902-26
	Haynes	Haynes Automobile Co.	1904-25
	Haynes-Apperson	Haynes-Apperson Auto. Co.	1898-1904
	Jack Rabbit	Apperson Bros. Auto. Co.	1911-13
Lafayette	American Junior	American Motor Vehicle Co.	1916-20
	Auto Red Bug	American Motor Vehicle Co.	1916-20
	Honda Passport	Subaru Isuzu Automotive, Inc.	1994-present
	Isuzu Trooper	Subaru Isuzu Automotive, Inc.	1989-present
	Mills Electric	Mills Electric Co.	1917
	Subaru Legacy	Subaru Isuzu Automotive, Inc.	1989-present
Lawrenceburg	Dearborn	J & M Motor Car Co.	1911
	James	J & M Motor Car Co.	1909-11
Ligonier	Mier	Mier Carriage & Buggy Co.	1908-09
Logansport	Bendix	Bendix Co.	1908-09
	Duplex	Bendix Co.	1908-09
	ReVere	ReVere Motor Car Corp.	1918-26
Marion	Crosley	Crosley Motors Inc.	1946-52

McCordsville	Leader	Leader Mfg. Co.	1905-07
Mishawaka	American Simplex	Simplex Motor Car Co.	1906-10
	Amplex	Simplex Motor Car Co.	1910-13
	Hummer	AM General	1984-present
	Kenworthy	Kenworthy Motors Corp.	1920-21
Muncie	Durant	Durant Motors, Inc.	1922-28
	Interstate	Interstate Motor Co.	1908-19
	Rider-Lewis	Rider-Lewis Motor Car Co.	1908
	Sheridan	Sheridan Motor Car Co.	1920-21
	Star	Durant Motors, Inc.	1923
New Albany	American	American Automobile Mfg. Co.	1911-12
	Hercules	Hercules Motor Car Co.	1914-15
	Jonz	American Automobile Mfg. Co.	1910-12
	Ohio Falls	Ohio Falls Motor Car Co.	1913-14
	Pilgrim	Ohio Falls Motor Car Co.	1913-14
New Castle	Maxwell	Maxwell-Briscoe Motor Co.	1906-16
	Lawter	Safety Shredder Co.	1909
N. Manchester	DeWitt	DeWitt Motor Vehicle Co.	1909-10
Peru	Bryan Steamer	Bryan Boiler Co.	1918-23
	Great Western	Great Western Automobile Co.	1909-14
	Model	Model Automobile Co.	1906-09
	Star	Model Automobile Co.	1908
Richmond	Crosley	Crosley Motors Inc.	1939-42
	Davis	George W. Davis Motor Car Co.	1908-29
	Laurel	Laurel Motor Car Co.	1916-17
	Lorraine	Lorraine Car Co.	1920-21
	New York Six	Automotive Corp. of America	1927-28
	Pilot	Pilot Motor Car Co.	1909-24
	Richmond	Wayne Works	1904-17
	Rodefeld	Rodefeld Co.	1909-17
	Seidel	Seidel Buggy Co.	1908-09
	Westcott	Westcott Motor Car Co.	1909-16
Ridgeville	Senator	Victor Automobile Co.	1907-10
Shelbyville	Clark	Clark Motor Car Co.	1910-12

South Bend	Avanti	Studebaker Corp.	1962-63
	Avanti II	Avanti Motor Corp.	1965-85
	Casady	W.S. Casady Mfg. Co.	1905
	Erskine	Studebaker Corp.	1927-30
	Packard	Studebaker-Packard Corp.	1954-58
	R.A.C.	Ricketts Automobile Co.	1910-11
	Ricketts	Ricketts Automobile Co.	1909-11
	Rockne	Studebaker Corp.	1932-33
	South Bend	South Bend Motor Car Works	1913-16
	Studebaker	Studebaker Corp.	1904-63
	Studebaker Elect.	Studebaker Bros. Mfg. Co.	1902-12
	Tincher	Tincher Motor Car Co.	1907-09
Terre Haute	Overland	Standard Wheel Works	1903-05
Union City	Union	Union Automobile Co.	1902-04
	Union City Six	Union City Carriage Mfg. Co.	1916
Vincennes	Dixie	Dixie Mfg. Co.	1916
Wabash	Champion	Champion Auto Equipment Co.	1916
	Standard Six	Standard Automobile Co. of America	1910-11
Woodburn	W.A.C.	Woodburn Auto Co.	1905-12
	Woodburn	Woodburn Auto Co.	1905-12

A word about lists

Compiling lists about the automotive genesis is an imprecise art. There is no single source of information for the American automobiles' progression. Some reference works are fairly complete regarding makes, manufacturers, cities and dates. These same works may miss some instances for which a manufacturer's model is built in a plant other than that company's main places of business. The work is further compounded by list compilers who chose to include instances where only one car was made by an individual whether or not they planned to proceed to manufacture it in quantity. In Indiana's case, for every one vehicle achieving production about two announcements of intent to manufacture or build a prototype were proclaimed.

Early lists about the actual number of automobiles made in the United States started at 1,500 and then progressed to about 2,500. Recent lists approach around 3,000. Early Indiana lists started at 160 makes made in more than 30 cities and have progressed to over 520 vehicles manufactured or assembled in more than 80 cities.

Only those vehicles which proceeded to production are included in this book's lists. Production, as we have chosen to define it, is the manufacture of 12 or more vehicles of the same design. This is the accepted definition for recognizing the start of commercial automobile production by a number of manufacturers in the United States in 1896. In some instances it is still hard to determine the twelve or greater number. On borderline cases where no actual numbers are given we erred on the high side. Based on the above explanation, this list shows 198 autos produced in 42 cities.

Indiana-built automobiles sorted by name

Name	Manufacturer	City	Date
Albany	Albany Automobile Co.	Albany	1907-08
Allied	Allied Cab Mfg. Co.	Elkhart	1932-34
American	American Motors Co.	Indianapolis	1906-14
American	American Automobile Mfg. Co.	New Albany	1911-12
American Junior	American Motor Vehicle Co.	Lafayette	1916-20
American Simplex	Simplex Motor Car Co.	Mishawaka	1906-10
American Underslung	American Motors Co.	Indianapolis	1906-14
Amplex	Simplex Motor Car Co.	Mishawaka	1910-13
Anderson	Anderson Carriage Mfg. Co.	Anderson	1907-10
Anderson Steam	Anderson Steam Carriage Co.	Anderson	1901-02
Ansted	Lexington Motor Car Co.	Connersville	1921, 1926
Apperson	Apperson Bros. Automobile Co.	Kokomo	1902-26
Auburn	Auburn Automobile Co.	Auburn	1900-36
Auburn	Auburn Automobile Co.	Connersville	1929-36
Auburn Motor Chassis	Auburn Motor Chassis Co.	Auburn	1912-15
Auto Red Bug	American Motor Vehicle Co.	Lafayette	1916-20
Avanti	Studebaker Corp.	South Bend	1962-63
Avanti II	Avanti Motor Corp.	South Bend	1965-85
Bendix	Bendix Co.	Logansport	1908-09
Black	C.H. Black Mfg. Co.	Indianapolis	1896-1900
Black Crow	Crow Motor Car Co.	Elkhart	1909-11
Blackhawk	Stutz Motor Car Co.	Indianapolis	1929-30
Bour-Davis	Shadburne Bros. Co.	Frankfort	1918
Brook Spacke	Machine & Tool Co.	Indianapolis	1920-21
Bryan Steamer	Bryan Boiler Co.	Peru	1918-23
Butler High Wheel	Butler Co.	Butler	1908
Casady	W.S. Casady Mfg. Co.	South Bend	1905
Champion	Champion Auto Equipment Co.	Wabash	1916
Chevrolet Truck	General Motors Truck & Bus Grp.	Fort Wayne	1986-present
Clark	Clark Motor Car Co.	Shelbyville	1910-12
Cole	Cole Motor Car Co.	Indianapolis	1909-25
Cole Solid Tire	Cole Carriage Co.	Indianapolis	1908-09
Comet	Comet Cyclecar Co.	Indianapolis	1914
Comet Racer	Marion Motor Car Co.	Indianapolis	1904

Continental	Indian Motor & Mfg. Co.	Franklin	1910-13
Cord	Cord Corp.	Auburn	1929-32
Cord	Cord Corp.	Connersville	1936-37
Crosley	Crosley Motors Inc.	Marion	1946-52
Crosley	Crosley Motors Inc.	Richmond	1939-42
Crow	Crow Motor Car Co.	Elkhart	1911
Crow-Elkhart	Crow Motor Car Co.	Elkhart	1911-23
Cyclop	L. Porter Smith & Bros.	Indianapolis	1910
Davis	George W. Davis Motor Car Co.	Richmond	1908-29
De Soto	Zimmerman Mfg. Co.	Auburn	1913-14
De Tamble	De Tamble Motor Co.	Anderson	1908-13
Dearborn	J & M Motor Car Co.	Lawrenceburg	1911
Decatur	Decatur Motor Car Co.	Decatur	1908-11
DeWitt	DeWitt Motor Vehicle Co.	North Manchester	1909-10
Dixie	Dixie Mfg. Co.	Vincennes	1916
Duesenberg	Duesenberg Motors Corp.	Indianapolis	1920-37
Duplex	Bendix Co.	Logansport	1908-09
Durant	Durant Motors, Inc.	Muncie	1922-28
El-Fay	Elkhart Motor Co.	Elkhart	1931-35
Elcar	Elkhart Motor Co.	Elkhart	1916-31
Electrobile	National Vehicle Co.	Indianapolis	1901-06
Elgin	Elgin Motors Inc.	Indianapolis	1923-24
Empire	Empire Motor Car Co.	Indianapolis	1909-19
Empire	Empire Motor Car Co.	Connersville	1912-15
Erie	Erie Cycle & Motor Carriage Co.	Anderson	1899-1902
Erskine	Studebaker Corp.	South Bend	1927-30
Evansville	Evansville Automobile Co.	Evansville	1907-09
Excellent Six	Rider-Lewis Motor Car Co.	Anderson	1908-11
Ford	Ford Motor Co.	Indianapolis	1914-32
Gary Six	Gary Automobile Mfg. Co.	Gary	1914
Graham-Paige	Graham-Paige	Evansville	1929-30
Great Western	Great Western Automobile Co.	Peru	1909-14
H.C.S.	H.C.S. Motor Co.	Indianapolis	1920-25
H.C.S. Cab	H.C.S. Cab Mfg. Co.	Indianapolis	1924-27
Handy Wagon	Auburn Motor Chassis Co.	Auburn	1912-15
Harper	Harper Buggy Co.	Columbia City	1907-08
Haynes	Haynes Automobile Co.	Kokomo	1904-25
Haynes-Apperson	Haynes-Apperson Automobile Co.	Kokomo	1898-1904
Henderson	Henderson Motor Car Co.	Indianapolis	1912-14
Hercules	Hercules Motor Car Co.	New Albany	1914-15
Herff-Brooks	Herff-Brooks Corp.	Indianapolis	1915-16
Honda Passport	Subaru Isuzu Automotive, Inc.	Lafayette	1994-present

Hoosier Scout	Warren Electric & Machine Co.	Indianapolis	1914
Howard	Lexington-Howard Co.	Connersville	1913-14
Huffman	Huffman Bros. Motor Co.	Elkhart	1920-25
Hummer	AM General	Mishawaka	1984-present
Huntingburg	Huntingburg Wagon Works	Huntingburg	1902-03
Ideal	Ideal Motor Co.	Indianapolis	1911-12
Ideal-Commercial	Ideal Auto Co.	Fort Wayne	1910-14
Imp	W. H. McIntyre Co.	Auburn	1913-14
Indiana	Indiana Motor & Vehicle Co.	Indianapolis	1901
Interstate	Interstate Motor Co.	Muncie	1908-19
Isuzu Trooper	Subaru Isuzu Automotive, Inc.	Lafayette	1989-present
Jack Rabbit	Apperson Bros. Automobile Co.	Kokomo	1911-13
James	J & M Motor Car Co.	Lawrenceburg	1909-11
Jonz	American Automobile Mfg. Co.	New Albany	1910-12
Kenworthy	Kenworthy Motors Corp.	Mishawaka	1920-21
Kiblinger	W. H. Kiblinger Co.	Auburn	1907-08
Komet	Elkhart Motor Car Co.	Elkhart	1911
Lafayette	Lafayette Motors Co.	Indianapolis	1921-22
Lambert	Buckeye Mfg. Co.	Anderson	1906-17
Laurel	Laurel Motors Corp.	Anderson	1917-20
Laurel	Laurel Motor Car Co.	Richmond	1916-17
Lawter	Safety Shredder Co.	New Castle	1909
Leader	Leader Mfg. Co.	Knightstown	1907-12
Leader	Leader Mfg. Co.	McCordsville	1905-07
Lexington	Lexington Motor Co.	Connersville	1910-27
Lindsay	T.J. Lindsay Automobile Parts Co.	Indianapolis	1902-03
Lorraine	Lorraine Car Co.	Richmond	1920-21
Lyons-Knight	Lyons-Atlas Co.	Indianapolis	1913-15
Madison	Madison Motors Corp.	Anderson	1915-19
Mais	Mais Motor Truck Co.	Indianapolis	1911-14
Marathon	Herff-Brooks Corp.	Indianapolis	1915-16
Marion	Marion Motor Car Co.	Indianapolis	1904-14
Marmon	Nordyke & Marmon Co.	Indianapolis	1902-33
Martel	Elkhart Motor Co.	Elkhart	1925-27
Martindale & Millikan	Indian Motor & Mfg. Co.	Franklin	1914
Maxwell	Maxwell-Briscoe Motor Co.	New Castle	1906-16
McFarlan	McFarlan Motor Car Co.	Connersville	1910-28
McGill	McGee Mfg. Co.	Indianapolis	1917-28
McIntyre	W. H. McIntyre Co.	Auburn	1909-15
McIntyre Special	W. H. McIntyre Co.	Auburn	1911-15
Merz	Merz Cyclecar Co.	Indianapolis	1914
Mier	Mier Carriage & Buggy Co.	Ligonier	1908-09
Mills Electric	Mills Electric Co.	Lafayette	1917

Model	Model Gas Engine Works	Auburn	1903-06
Model	Model Automobile Co.	Peru	1906-09
Mohawk	Mohawk Cycle & Automobile Co.	Indianapolis	1903-05
Monroe	William Small Co.	Indianapolis	1918-23
Morriss-London	Century Motors Co.	Elkhart	1919-25
Muntz Jet	Muntz Car Co.	Evansville	1950-51
National	National Motor Vehicle Co.	Indianapolis	1904-24
National Electric	National Automobile & Electric Co.	Indianapolis	1900-04
New Parry	Parry Auto Co.	Indianapolis	1911-12
New York Six	Automotive Corp. of America	Richmond	1927-28
Niagara Four	Crow Motor Car Co.	Elkhart	1915-16
Nyberg	Nyberg Automobile Works	Anderson	1911-13
Ohio Falls	Ohio Falls Motor Car Co.	New Albany	1913-14
Overland	Standard Wheel Works	Indianapolis	1905-06
Overland	Overland Auto Co.	Indianapolis	1906-09
Overland	Standard Wheel Works	Terre Haute	1903-05
Packard	Studebaker-Packard Corp.	South Bend	1954-58
Packard Darrin	Packard Motor Car Co.	Connersville	1940-41
Pak-Age-Car	Auburn Automobile Co.	Connersville	1938-41
Pak-Age-Car	Stutz Motor Co.	Indianapolis	1930-38
Parry	Parry Auto Co.	Indianapolis	1910
Pathfinder	Motor Car Mfg. Co.	Indianapolis	1912-17
Pilgrim	Ohio Falls Motor Car Co.	New Albany	1913-14
Pilot	Pilot Motor Car Co.	Richmond	1909-24
Plymouth	Chrysler Corp.	Evansville	1935-56
Pope-Waverly	Pope Motor Car Co.	Indianapolis	1904-08
Postal	Postal Auto. & Engineering Co.	Bedford	1906-08
Pratt	Pratt Motor Car Co.	Elkhart	1911-15
Pratt-Elkhart	Elkhart Carriage/Harness Mfg. Co.	Elkhart	1909-11
Premier	Premier Motor Mfg. Co.	Indianapolis	1903-26
Premier Taxicab	Premier Motor Car Co.	Indianapolis	1923-26
Prosperity	Allied Cab Mfg. Co.	Elkhart	1933
R.A.C.	Ricketts Automobile Co.	South Bend	1910-11
Red Ball-Taxi	Red Ball Transit Co.	Frankfort	1924
Reeves	Reeves Pulley Co.	Columbus	1896-98 1905
ReVere	ReVere Motor Car Corp.	Logansport	1918-26
Richmond	Wayne Works	Richmond	1904-17
Ricketts	Ricketts Automobile Co.	South Bend	1909-11
Rider-Lewis	Rider-Lewis Motor Car Co.	Anderson	1908-11
Rider-Lewis	Rider-Lewis Motor Car Co.	Muncie	1908
Rockne	Studebaker Corp.	South Bend	1932-33
Rodefeld	Rodefeld Co.	Richmond	1909-17
Roosevelt	Marmon Motor Car Co.	Indianapolis	1929-30
Royal	Royal Motor Co.	Elkhart	1913

Royal Martel	Elkhart Motor Co.	Elkhart	1925-27
Scout	International Harvester Co.	Fort Wayne	1961-80
Seidel	Seidel Buggy Co.	Richmond	1908-09
Senator	Victor Automobile Co.	Ridgeville	1907-10
Sheridan	Sheridan Motor Car Co.	Muncie	1920-21
Shoemaker	Shoemaker Automobile Co.	Elkhart	1907-08
Simplicity	Evansville Automobile Co.	Evansville	1907-11
Single-Center	Single-Center Buggy Co.	Evansville	1906-08
South Bend	South Bend Motor Car Works	South Bend	1913-16
Spacke	Spacke Machine & Tool Co.	Indianapolis	1919
Standard Six	Standard Auto. Co. of America	Wabash	1910-11
Star	Durant Motors, Inc.	Muncie	1923
Star	Model Automobile Co.	Peru	1908
Sterling	Elkhart Motor Car Co.	Elkhart	1909-11
Studebaker	Studebaker Corp.	South Bend	1904-63
Studebaker Electric	Studebaker Bros. Mfg. Co.	South Bend	1902-12
Stutz	Stutz Motor Car Co.	Indianapolis	1912-35
Subaru Legacy	Subaru Isuzu Automotive, Inc.	Lafayette	1989-present
Sun	Sun Motor Car Co.	Elkhart	1916-17
Super Allied	Allied Cab Mfg. Co.	Elkhart	1935
Tincher	Tincher Motor Car Co.	South Bend	1907-09
Traveler	Traveler Automobile Co.	Evansville	1910-11
Tricolet	Pokorney/Richards Auto. & Gas.	Indianapolis	1904-06
Union	Union Automobile Co.	Auburn	1916
Union	Buckeye Mfg. Co.	Anderson	1905
Union	Union Automobile Co.	Union City	1902-04
Union City Six	Union City Carriage Mfg. Co.	Union City	1916
United	United Engineering Co.	Greensburg	1919-20
Van Auken Electric	Connersville Buggy Co.	Connersville	1913
W.A.C.	Woodburn Auto Co.	Woodburn	1905-12
Waverly	Waverly Co.	Indianapolis	1909-16
Waverly Electric	Indiana Bicycle Co.	Indianapolis	1898-1903
Westcott	Westcott Motor Car Co.	Richmond	1909-16
Woodburn	Woodburn Auto Co.	Woodburn	1905-12

Index